DAVID HOHNEN

Hamlet's Castle and Shakespeare's Elsinore

Christian Ejlers
Copenhagen

HAMLET'S CASTLE AND
SHAKESPEARE'S ELSINORE

Copyright © David Hohnen 2000
ISBN 87 7241 028 0

First published 2000
Reprinted 2001
Second edition 2004

Cover photo: Arne Magnussen

Design and typesetting: Zakrisson,
www.polytype.dk, Copenhagen
Typefaces: Poliphilus and Blado

Litho reproduction and printing:
Narayana Press, Gylling, Denmark

Distributed in the UK and Ireland by
Vine House Distribution Ltd
Waldenbury, Chailey
East Sussex BN8 4DR
England
sales@vinehouseuk.co.uk

Danish edition
HAMLET, KRONBORG OG
SHAKESPEARES HELSINGØR
ISBN 87 7241 360 3

Christian Ejlers' Forlag
Sølvgade 38/3
DK 1307 Copenhagen K
Denmark
liber@ce-publishers.dk

Acknowledgements

I am most grateful to the Velux Foundation of 1981
for a generous grant towards the cost of publishing this
book. I also thank all those who have kindly helped and
advised me in various ways, especially the Hon. Fionn
Morgan, Col. John E. Zilmer, Steward of Kronborg
Castle, and Hanne Poulsen, Librarian of the Handels-
og Søfartsmuseum at Kronborg Castle. My greatest
debt of thanks, however, is to Dr Thorkild Kjærgaard,
who has not only read my typescript critically and piloted
me through some of the more hazardous waters of
Danish historiography, but also given me sound advice and
encouragement in matters far beyond the strictly historical.

D. H.

NOTE Line citations from *Hamlet* are taken from
the Arden Shakespeare edition by Harold Jenkins,
1982 (1995); references to other plays by Shakespeare
follow The Annotated Shakespeare edited by
A.L. Rowse, 1978.

Contents

PART ONE

Waters flowing with gold

Why Elsinore?

The thousands of visitors who flock to Elsinore every year to see 'Hamlet's Castle' – even in the bleak mid-winter – may be forgiven for assuming that this little Danish town must owe its fame to Shakespeare. But in one sense it was almost the other way round.

It is perhaps understandable that Shakespeare should have rejected the bleak moorlands of Jutland (which is where the original Hamlet legend is said to have taken place) but if he needed a more colourful setting for his tragedy about a prince at the royal court of Denmark, surely Copenhagen would have been a more natural choice? After all, Copenhagen was the Danish capital, had its own medieval castle and had been the royal seat of Danish kings ever since the middle of the fifteenth century. What made him prefer Elsinore?

To start with, Elsinore was already so famous in its own right in Shakespeare's time that many people believed that it was actually the capital of Denmark. There was a special reason for this. During the last quarter of the sixteenth century Denmark was the most powerful Continental kingdom in Northern Europe and as such constantly engaged in diplomatic activities, particularly with England. But visiting Denmark in the winter was not always an enjoyable experience. Ambassadors, emissaries and their retinues therefore preferred to travel when the weather was pleasanter, and it was well known that during the summertime the Danish king, Frederik II, spent much of his time at Elsinore, where he had recently converted an old medieval naval fortress into a magnificent palace in the Dutch Renaissance style, complete with splendid towers, elegant spires, rich sculptural ornamentation and even a huge ballroom that was acknowledged to be the largest in northern Europe. That he had reportedly done so partly to indulge his young queen, Sophie, who happened to be very fond of dancing, only added to the general awe and admiration.

Trumpeter. Detail of engraving, *c.* 1590.

Engraving after a drawing by Hans Knieper *c.* 1582 showing the town of Elsinore, the Castle (Kronenburg) and the old Custom House (Olde Tolbod).

The unique position of this castle at Elsinore, guarding the entrance to (and exit from) the Baltic on a narrow spit of land jutting out into the sea just where the straits between Denmark and what is now Sweden are at their narrowest, a mere four kilometres, was in itself unusually dramatic.

Numerous reports had been circulated by diplomats, merchants, travellers, sailors and many others who had visited the town about the magnificence of the Danish court at Elsinore and the extraordinary forms of lavishness displayed there. There were lurid stories about the heavy drinking that took place, frequently accompanied by what had become known as 'cannon-healths'. It was well known that at formal banquets, every time a glass was raised (as often as not the King's) and a toast proposed, the kettle-drums would roll, the trumpets would sound, and outside on the ramparts the artillerymen would respond to the signal by firing ear-blasting volleys of shot. Shakespeare refers to this custom in the first act of *Hamlet* when the King says:

No jocund health that Denmark drinks today
But the great cannon to the clouds shall tell,
And the King's rouse the heaven shall bruit again,
Re-speaking earthly thunder.*

(I.ii.125–28)

and again when Hamlet, Horatio and Marcellus are on the battlements and a flourish of trumpets and cannon shots are heard:

The King doth wake tonight and takes his rouse,
…
And as he drains his draughts of Rhenish down,
The kettle-drum and the trumpet thus bray out
The triumph of his pledge

(I.iv.7–11)

* **jocund** merry
  Denmark the King
  of Denmark
  rouse toast
  bruit proclaim

Towards the end of the play, just before the fatal duel starts, Shakespeare describes this specifically Danish custom in even greater detail. The King orders the cups of wine to be placed before him in readiness and then declares:

> Let all the battlements their ordnance fire:
>
> …
>
> And let the kettle to the trumpet speak,
> The trumpet to the cannoneer without,
> The cannons to the heavens, the heavens to earth,
> 'Now the King drinks to Hamlet.'
>
> (V.ii.267–275)

In addition to the reports Shakespeare had apparently heard about this colourful ritual he might well have seen drawings of the castle at Elsinore and even a description of it in an illustrated atlas such as that published in Cologne in Latin by Braunius and Hohenbergius in 1585–86 and entitled *Civitates Orbis Terrarum* (The Cities of the World), in which the Danish King's extravagantly rebuilt castle was praised for being

> an unassailable fortress which, with admirable ingenuity, has been fortified to such a degree that only those who are weary of life would ever think of attacking it [...] a splendidly beautiful building whose roofs and spires glow in the sunshine like gold, and where elaborate tapestries, a magnificent fountain and royal tournaments inevitably fill the beholder with astonishment.

How had all this extravagance been possible? Where did the Danish King's wealth come from? The chronicler gave a hint:

> Denmark, which owns no gold mines, does however possess something no less valuable in the Sound,* whose waters flow with gold, for all ships must pay toll in gold to the King, who in return, by preventing the ungodly assaults of pirates, reserves the use of the sea for the benefit of merchants.

* The channel of water between Denmark and what is now Sweden.

A boy named Bugislav

The remarkable affluence of Denmark's monarchs had begun more than a hundred and fifty years earlier with the introduction of an arrangement that was to remain in force right up to the middle of the nineteenth century. Later historians have described it with some astonishment and a touch of admiration as "400 years of legal piracy".

The king behind this achievement is known in Danish history books as Erik of Pomerania, or – even more confusingly – as Erik VII of Pomerania, although he was never king of Pomerania at all, nor even named Erik in the first place. When he was a little boy his parents called him Bugislav. He came into the picture rather unexpectedly.

At the end of the fourteenth century, Denmark, Norway and Sweden had become united under a woman, Queen Margrete, daughter of the previous Danish king, Valdemar Atterdag.

It had been an unusual course of events. On her father's death in 1375 Margrete, then aged twenty-two, was married to the king of Norway, Haakon, with whom she had a five-year-old son, Olav. Her father had died without leaving a male heir. At first it seemed natural to elect the son of his eldest daughter, Ingeborg, but Margrete, who had already displayed talent as a negotiator, succeeded in getting her own son elected on the understanding that she and her husband would act as his regents until he came of age. But five years later Haakon also died, whereupon Olav inherited the kingdom of Norway as well. Margrete

Alabaster effigy of Margrete I on her sarcophagus in Roskilde Cathedral.

Document dated 10 August 1387 confirming Queen Margrete's election as ruler of Denmark and all its lands. Contemporary annals recorded that it was "because of the wisdom which God hath given her". Fourteen signatories – bishops, knights and esquires – appended their seals.

proposed that she should simply continue to rule both kingdoms as his regent, which was also accepted.

Margrete was never actually crowned but simply hailed by the nobles of Denmark and Norway as "Empowered Mistress and Master and Guardian of the Whole Kingdom of Denmark". After protract‑ ed negotiations with Swedish noblemen and finally defeating the Swedish army in battle, she also became ruler of Sweden.

But then, suddenly and most disconcertingly, Olav also died. Margrete was faced with a serious problem. Realizing that her dream of a Scandinavian union was endangered, she devised an ingenious solution. She happened to have a niece who was married to the Duke of Pomerania in the north of Germany. This couple had a little boy aged six named Bugislav, and Margrete, after explaining her predicament, persuaded them to let her adopt him.

She realized that her Scandinavian countrymen might not take kindly to the thought of having a king with a Slavonic name, so she promptly changed it to Erik. She knew this would be more acceptable, for there had already been six previous Eriks on the throne of Den‑ mark.

The United Kingdom
of Scandinavia,
1397–1448

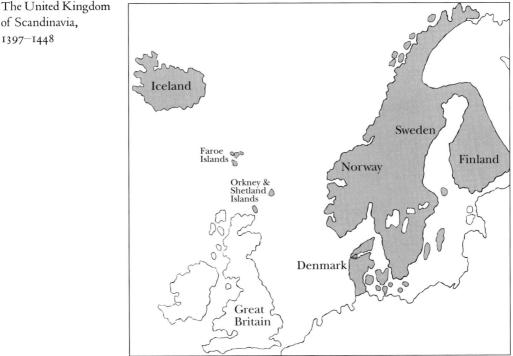

Margrete then travelled round the three countries with her con-
veniently adopted little boy and had him hailed as king in many places.
Finally, in 1397, she summoned a convention of the nobles of all three
kingdoms at what was then the border town of Kalmar in the south-
east of Sweden.

Margrete was a firm believer in Scandivanian unity. She felt it should
be simple to achieve provided certain elementary principles were
observed: the Scandinavian countries should have a common monarch
(preferably her adopted son), a common defence policy (in the event of
any one of them being attacked by an enemy, the other two must come
to its support) and all three countries should agree to be ruled by their
own respective laws without interference.

Agreement was formally reached that the three kingdoms were to be
united under one king, to be elected jointly, whereupon the so-called
Kalmar Union became a reality. Erik was duly elected and then
crowned King of all Scandinavia. But he was still only fifteen, so
Margrete continued to rule the three kingdoms on his behalf.

Even when he came of age, Margrete saw no reason to relinquish her
authority. Prior to his departure for Norway on one specific mission she

gave him a detailed list of 54 instructions (the document is still preserved, dated November 1404) telling him precisely what he was to do
and how he was to conduct himself. It was not until she died in 1412
that Erik, by this time aged thirty, at last found himself the sole ruler of
the United Kingdom of Scandinavia.

It was vast: in addition to Denmark (which then included several
provinces in the south of what is now Sweden), Norway and Sweden
(which at the time included the whole of what is now Finland)
it extended westwards to include the Orkney and Shetland Islands
(not annexed by Scotland until 1472), northwards to Spitsbergen
and southwards to include what much later became the duchies of
Schleswig and Holstein in northern Germany.

All the King's fish

Erik was faced with many difficulties, especially in finding enough
money to meet his huge administrative expenses. Admittedly he had
several sources of income, one of the most considerable (and remarkable) being the herring fisheries concentrated off the south-western
coast of the Scandinavian peninsula. However, despite having long
been a seemingly inexhaustible source of revenue for the royal Danish
purse, it seemed to be slipping slowly through his fingers, for since the
turn of the century the herring shoals, for unknown reasons, had been
gradually moving further north.

Woodcut in Olaus
Magnus, *Historia de
gentibus septentrionalibus*
(1555), Book 20,
Chapter 28, illustrating
the 'miraculous' density
of the herring shoals
in the Sound.

1:1

The herring fisheries of southern Scandinavia had caused amazement for a long time. In the twelfth century, a French eyewitness,
Philippe de Maizières, described what he called two 'miracles'. The
first was the fact that the shoals of herring passing through the Sound
every year were so densely packed that "one can scarce row a boat
through them ... they may be scooped up by hand without the use of
nets". The second was that in his estimation

> every year some 40,000 boats gather in these waters, each with a
> crew of at least six men, sometimes eight or ten; in addition, at
> least 500 other large vessels occupy themselves solely with the
> task of salting all the herring caught by the fishing boats.

Maizières was quite sure that these enormous catches of herring
represented a demonstration of God's infinite grace and divine mercy,
for it meant that during the difficult period of Lent the entire popu-
lations of France, Germany, England and many other countries had
enough to eat. As he said: "Poor folk can always afford a herring, even
if larger fish are beyond their means." His estimate (perhaps rather
wild) was that during the two months or so the season lasted, about
300,000 people were engaged in the herring trade – catching, cleaning,
salting or selling – and they all paid their taxes or licence fees to the
Danish King.

One English 'noble'

Erik was aware, however, that God's mercy could not be expected to
last for ever. Plans were forming in his mind, and in 1423 he finally
summoned to Copenhagen a group of merchants from the powerful
German Hanseatic League, which at the time dominated nearly all
trade in northern Europe. He informed them that henceforth he intended
to levy a new toll: every ship wishing to sail past Elsinore, whether on
its way out of or into the Baltic, would have to dip its flag, strike its
topsails and cast anchor so that the captain might go ashore and pay to
the customs officers in the town a toll of 'one English noble'.*

Nobody challenged the right of the King of all Scandinavia to
impose a toll of this kind. After all, mere barons who owned castles on
the banks of the Rhine, the Danube and other major European water-
ways had for centuries forced all passing ships to pay a similar toll.

* A noble was a gold coin
first minted by Edward III
of England in the fourteenth
century and so named
because of the superiority of
its gold. It was thus a strong
and respected currency.
This was important, because
at this time the Scandinavian
and Baltic currencies were
unstable and rates of
exchange tended to fluctuate
disturbingly. At the time its
purchasing value corre-
sponded to about one ox.
From 1465 it bore a stylized
picture of a rose and then
became known as a 'rose
noble'.

Fifteenth-century
English nobles
(actual size).

However, its relative heaviness, combined with the obligation to cast anchor at Elsinore in order to hand over the money, made it highly unpopular.

In order to assert his authority and deter skippers from trying to slip past without paying, Erik was aware that he would have to to build a strong castle and arm it with as many guns as possible. The town's geographical position was admirable for this purpose. Its anglicized name, Elsinore, is an internationally recognized version of the Danish name, Helsingør, which derives from the old Danish word *hælsingar*, meaning inhabitants close to a *hals*, or neck. This is a reference to the fact that at this point the straits virtually represent a bottle-neck. The fairway itself is even narrower and shaped like an elbow, which means that any ship, whether coming from the North Sea and bound for the Baltic, or north-bound and wishing to leave it, must change course abruptly in order to pass Elsinore. At the time, this often entailed heaving to and waiting for a favourable wind. There were admittedly two other routes through the Danish islands, the Great Belt and the Little Belt, but the former was full of dangerous banks and the latter was very narrow and moreover had a strong current. There was no restriction on using these routes, but the same toll had to be paid as in the Sound.

Erik foresaw that if he also established a proper town at Elsinore, sea-captains, after paying their toll and then waiting for a favourable wind, would welcome an opportunity to replenish stocks of water, wine, meat, vegetables and whatever else they needed. In other words, even if they had to pay toll, calling in at Elsinore could have its attractions – all he had to do was provide them.

A new fortress

The site Erik chose was Krogen (literally 'the hook') a spit of land just north of the town, and he gave his castle the same name. He could hardly have found a bolder or more strategic position, for its guns were able to cover the surrounding waters through an impressively sweeping arc of 265°. In combination with another medieval castle with a mighty donjon on the eastern side of the strait, he would be able – at least in theory – to exercise supreme control of the gateway to the Baltic.

Contemporary drawing of three powerful monarchs who met in Hungary at Buda in 1424: the Byzantine Emperor Johannes VIII Paleologus; the German King Sigismund; and (right) Erik of Pomerania, King of the United Kingdom of Scandinavia.

Krogen was an extremely solid, completely square building. Each side of its curtain wall measured 120 ells (about 79 metres). This wall was some ten metres high, four metres thick facing inland, slightly less than two metres thick facing the sea and crowned by a parapet with openings through which boiling water, tar and other deterrents could be dropped. The war machines of the period – such as trebuchets, capable of slinging big boulders – stood little chance of doing any serious damage. By the time the castle was completed, it was regarded, especially by those who observed it from the sea as they passed, as an awesome manifestation of strength and invincibility. Its purpose was clear to all: it demonstrated the incontestable power of the King of all Scandinavia.

Erik must have finished building Krogen Castle by 1427, for in a letter dated 28 June that same year (still preserved) and addressed to the Prussian Grand Master Paul von Russdorf, he expressed his annoyance. He had been informed, he wrote, that a fleet of ships coming from the north, some of them Prussian, "when sailing past my castle, had had the temerity to shoot at it with its guns in a hostile manner".

The piracy problem

Medieval herring barrel.

To make his toll scheme more acceptable to seafaring nations, Erik realized that he must offer some attractive advantages in return. One of these was the assurance that he would do his best to keep his waters free of pirates. He would establish special patrols to keep an eye on all piratical activities, apprehend all pirates as fast as possible, and generally do whatever he could to make his waters safe; this included establishing a number of primitive lighthouse services.

Erik's so-called Sound Dues were to be paid at Elsinore, and all freebooters and pirates seized red-handed were to be taken to Elsinore for execution. They were to be broken on the wheel and then beheaded, after which their heads would be stuck on poles as a warning to all and confirmation that the King was keeping his part of the agreement. (Later they would just be hanged from a gallows and their bodies left to dangle ominously in the wind).

At this time piracy could be a profitable way of life, but when caught a pirate could expect no mercy. There was an occasion in Erik of Pomerania's time when over a hundred seamen, crews of a small fleet of pirate ships, were finally overpowered after attacking a merchantman. Every man was bound and stuffed into a herring cask, after which the lid was nailed on. The casks were then "stacked neatly, layer upon layer" in the hold; on reaching port, they were broken open one by one and each wretch taken out and strung up on a gallows.

Until far into the seventeenth century, piracy was a constant and considerable danger to shipping, but the introduction of the Sound Dues represented a certain degree of control, for every skipper was obliged to heave to and permit Danish customs officials to board and inspect his ship.

Pirates could expect no mercy. The various forms of punishment were also among the torments likely to be awaiting any sinner in Purgatory. Fresco in Aarhus Cathedral, Jutland, *c.* 1475–1500.

The Danish King's demonstration of his command of the sea was in itself a deterrent, but in the same way that kings who wished to wage war or defend their territories could always hire mercenaries to do the fighting on land, they could also hire privately owned ships, arm them and then commission them for war service. These so-called 'privateers' were then issued with a licence authorizing them to seize merchant vessels of another nation – and, of course, their cargoes.

Strictly speaking, both privateers and pirates spent their working lives attacking, boarding and plundering merchant vessels, but whereas the privateers were officially authorized to do so and had their king's blessing, pirates were obviously regarded as acting criminally. The problem was that it could sometimes be difficult to distinguish between an honourable privateer and a scoundrelly buccaneer. After all, both occupations employed the same tactics and both were highly profitable, with the result that a privateer might well be tempted to continue his good work even after the conclusion of peace – and it was not unheard of for a monarch to 'overlook' such regrettable practice in return for a clandestinely arranged share of the booty.

Elsinore's first charter

To encourage the development of the town itself, Erik granted Elsinore a municipal charter, virtually elevating it to the same status as Copenhagen. This document, dated 2 June 1426, has also been preserved. It is written in straightforward terms and has the King's wax seal attached to it. Erik enjoined his "dearly beloved citizens" to build a new quarter closer to the water. He promised to grant them special privileges. His terms were attractive: tax exemption for five years for building a wooden house, ten years for one built of brick and stone. With these incentives, Elsinore soon grew and expanded at what was an unusually rapid rate for the period.

Elsinore's modest prosperity had always been wholly dependent upon the sea. For centuries the townsfolk had engaged in the same basic professions of fishing, ferrying and piloting, but the introduction of the Sound Dues suddenly produced an unprecedented wave of affluence. One thing rapidly led to another. The fact that every skipper wishing to pass Elsinore in either direction had to cast anchor and go ashore to pay his dues immediately generated considerable paper work. Officials and clerks had to be appointed to handle it – and they all had to have somewhere to live. Every payment had to be received and noted, and the name and nationality of every ship had to be recorded. All skippers needed the services of pilots, ferrymen, shipchandlers, lightermen, sailmakers, ropemakers, carpenters and smiths. The population soon became extraordinarily cosmopolitan, for skippers preferred to deal with their own countrymen, and the best way to start was to find a tavern with the coat of arms of their native town – Amsterdam, London, Plymouth or wherever – hanging over the front door, for then they could always be sure to find someone who spoke their own language.

Skippers were also able to buy provisions of all kinds from the many wine-merchants, grocers, butchers, bakers and candlestick-makers who soon thronged into the town. In their wake followed tailors, hatters, shoemakers, taverners, harlots, cripples and beggars. At their respective levels, they all profited from the Sound Dues.

The cargoes carried by many of the ships calling in at Elsinore also proved to be of great interest. Exotic spices and perfumes, expensive silks and satins, strong German beer and fine wines – all were procurable from time to time. The King, his courtiers and other noblemen only had to send word to His Majesty's customs superintendent at Elsinore and offers would soon be forthcoming. Reports of this extraordinary situation, which enabled the King of Scandinavia to lay his hands on all manner of luxury goods, often at most advantageous prices, spread all over Europe. On one occasion they came to the ears of Charles V, the Holy Roman Emperor. On inquiring politely of a Danish admiral who had entered his service where the best vineyards were to be found in Denmark, the answer came promptly: "In Elsinore, Sire, the best in the world!"

No wonder the town grew and prospered, except in times of serious political unrest. However, there was another serious and frequently recurring threat: during severe winters the waters of the Sound sometimes became ice-bound, bringing all shipping to a standstill.

Whereas most towns evolve slowly and organically, the late medieval quarter of Elsinore is clearly the result of a plan that could have been sketched on a piece of paper, for it is virtually a geometrical pattern of streets intersecting one another at right angles. Erik of Pomerania may well have been personally responsible for this plan. Its base line was Stengade (Stone Street), which is still the town's main street, so named because in Erik's day it was the only street in the town to be paved with cobblestones. At right angles to Stengade was Torvestræde (Market Lane) which was used as a market place. It is now called Sankt Annagade (St Anne's Street). Other streets found their natural place in the angle between Stengade and Sankt Annagade.

They are all still there.

The protection of seafarers

There is no statue of Shakespeare in Elsinore. The one true benefactor acknowledged by the townspeople is Erik of Pomerania. A monument erected in the market square in 1926 to commemorate Elsinore's 500th anniversary features a statue of a determined young monarch on his throne clasping a roll of parchment to symbolize the privileges he granted the town in 1426. Engraved across the plinth are the words MIT HAAB STAAR TIL HAVET, which is the Danish version of the Latin *In mari spes mea* (I place my hope in the sea), said to have been his motto, though possibly not attributed to him until after his death. But it certainly reflected his whole outlook.

However, as a devout Catholic Erik knew that it was all very well placing his faith in the sea, but that his prosperity lay not so much 'in the lap of the gods' as in the hands of the Virgin Mary and a few saints acknowledged to be well-disposed towards seafarers.

Elsinore had had a parish church ever since the early thirteenth century, said to have been consecrated from the outset to St Olav, the patron saint of Norway, who was known to favour sailors. He had once been caught in a storm on a Norwegian lake, whereupon he fell to his knees on the deck of his ship, clasped his hands and made a holy vow: if God would protect him from this peril he, in turn, would promise to build a church in commemoration of his salvation. Many churches were built in Scandinavia in return for divine intervention of this kind, and many of them were dedicated to St Olav.

To strengthen his spiritual position even further Erik donated land to three orders of mendicant friars: the Carmelites, the Franciscans and the Dominicans. The Carmelites not only built a monastery in the heart of the town, close to the parish church, but also an additional church of their own right next to it, consecrated to the Virgin Mary. The Franciscans built a second monastery and consecrated it to St

St Gertrude. Fresco in Jetsmark Church, North Jutland. Her attribute is a church, symbolizing her convent at Nivelles in the province of Brabant, Belgium.

Northern cloister of the
Carmelite Monastery.

Anne, mother of the Virgin Mary, and the Dominicans a third, consecrated to the ever popular and dependable St Nicholas, who was the
patron saint of all sailors and travellers.*

So what with one saint and another, Erik did much for the protection of seafarers. Also highly popular was St Gertrude, widely
acknowledged to be the protector, more than any other saint, of "all
sailors and travellers". An external niche in the wall of a hospital built
by the Carmelites for foreign sailors indicates that it was intended for
an image of St Gertrude, for it was common practice to place a statue

* Whereas the Dominican
and Franciscan monasteries
were dissolved after the
Reformation, the Carmelite
monastery still stands in
Elsinore and is now one
of the best preserved in
northern Europe.

of her out of doors, facing the sea. In the harsh Scandinavian climate the polychrome would soon wear off, after which the Danish saying "the gilt has worn off St Gertrude" arose, in much the same sense as the English phrase "to rub the gilt off the gingerbread".

Two altars were dedicated to St Gertrude in the church of St Olav, and a St Gertrude's guild took upon itself to bury (and say masses for) any dead body washed ashore on this coastline. Anyone who set forth on a journey in these parts would always first drink a toast to St Gertrude, for it was firmly believed that she would be of help, not only on any journey in this life, but also on the final one after death.

Erik of Pomerania, having established a new source of income to relieve his dependence on the herring shoals and then also done every-thing in his power to promote Elsinore's prosperity and protect the seafarers upon whom his monarchy was so dependent, watched his project proceeding as he had hoped: Elsinore expanded and prospered.

An English Queen of Denmark

One of Erik's major political problems was to find a successor. His foster-mother Margrete had taken an initial practical step on his behalf many years previously. Anxious to arrange a suitable marriage for him, her choice fell on Philippa, daughter of Henry IV of England. Erik married this English princess by proxy in 1405. The following year the young couple met for the first time and celebrated a magnificent wedding at Lund Cathedral (in what today is southern Sweden) to which guests were invited from all over Scandinavia. The bridegroom was twenty-three and the bride was twelve.

But the years passed and their marriage remained childless, so Erik formed a new plan. He had a cousin in Pomerania – another Bugislav – and decided to make him his heir. He reasoned that if he could persuade him to marry Princess Hedvig, the heir to the Polish throne, he might be able to add Poland to his Scandinavian empire – Poland at this time included Lithuania, the Ukraine and Byelorussia.

With the aim of consolidating this extraordinarily ambitious scheme, Erik set out on a long journey, visiting many countries and foreign potentates, including Sigismund, the Holy Roman Emperor in Hungary, who agreed to his proposals. Erik apparently made a good impression at the court. A contemporary chronicler described him as

A drawing of Queen Philippa made in 1640 by Crispijn de Passe the Younger.

a handsome man with golden-yellow hair and a splendid
physique who could leap into a saddle at one bound without
the help of a stirrup [...] all women were drawn to him with a
most passionate yearning.

But then Princess Hedvig died, and that was the end of Erik's
dream.

Erik may have been handsome, golden-haired and athletic, but he
was also known to be impetuous and tactless – diplomacy was never
his strong point. The problems involved in ruling his far-flung kingdoms became increasingly burdensome. His harsh taxation policies led
to a rebellion in Sweden, and by 1439 his 'persistent stubbornness' (as
his behaviour was described) finally cost him all three crowns and all
three kingdoms; in the end he was virtually deposed, whereupon he
retired to the island of Gotland in the Baltic, which at the time was a
strong naval base. However, as he needed some alternative form of
income he turned, curiously enough, to piracy. After all, he was quite
familiar with the profession in one way or another, for according to
chroniclers even his father, the Duke of Pomerania, was reputed to be
'a great robber'. Perhaps it was a natural choice; at all events he plied
this old trade successfully for thirteen years before finally returning to
the land of his birth, Pomerania, where he died at the age of 77.

Meanwhile Elsinore – his life-work, gateway to the Baltic, guardian
of the Sound – continued to prosper, and the Sound Dues continued
to pour into the coffers of a long succession of Danish kings.

Although widely acknowledged to be a success – politically, econom-
ically and culturally – Queen Margrete's grandly conceived and hard-
won union of the Scandinavian countries was only to last 126 years,
having been gradually undermined by a persistent conflict of interests
between the monarchy and the aristocracy that culminated in Stockholm in 1520 when the Danish King, Christian II, caused more than
100 Swedish noblemen to be slaughtered on the executioner's block,
after which Sweden broke away from the union. The bitter state of
rivalry that developed between Sweden and the twin kingdoms of
Denmark and Norway in the wake of this massacre, known in Scandinavian history as the Stockholm Bloodbath, was to erupt in war after
war during the next two centuries.

The threat from Lübeck

Erik of Pomerania's old castle served its purpose for almost a hundred years, but during the first half of the sixteenth century Elsinore had a number of bad scares, the first being in 1512 when the town was attacked by a fleet sent by the powerful Hanseatic town of Lübeck; it was repulsed and Elsinore survived, but a more serious blow was to follow.

Crown Prince Christian, heir to the Danish throne, had spent many years as vice-regent in Norway, where he had fallen in love with a commoner, a Dutch girl named Dyveke whose widowed mother, Sigbrit Willumsdatter, earned her living by selling cakes and pastries. He made Dyveke his mistress and installed both her and her mother in his household. On his accession in 1513 as Christian II he took them both with him to Copenhagen.

In 1522 the Lübeckers attacked again. This time the people of Elsinore are said to have fled into the nearby forests. According to a contemporary account they were intent only "on saving as many of their worldly goods as possible". One can hardly blame them. The attackers then set fire to the town, which is why so relatively few early sixteenth-century houses have survived.

Mother Sigbritt (here depicted beside Christian II in a painting made in 1873 by Kristian Zahrtmann) displayed such exceptional financial talents that she soon became Christian's chief economic adviser. Within three years he had entrusted her with the administration of all toll revenues throughout Denmark and Norway, including the Sound Dues. Sigbrit Willumsdatter decided that these were far too important to be collected and administered in Elsinore and therefore transferred the Customs House to Copenhagen, whereupon Elsinore's prosperity came to an abrupt standstill. Fortunately for the townsfolk the arrangement was to last only a few years. Christian II lost his throne and was succeeded by his uncle, who as Frederik I restored the privilege to Elsinore and in due course moreover gave the town a signed declaration to the effect that this decision was to remain in force "forever and a day".

Christian II.
Detail of an altar-piece
probably by Michel Sit-
tow, 1515, formerly in
the Carmelite Church
of St Mary, Elsinore,
(now in National-
museet, Copenhagen)
portraying the Danish
King as a pious person.
After the Stockholm
Bloodbath he became
better known to the
Swedes as 'Christian
the Tyrant'.

During the 1530s Elsinore became embroiled in a peculiar political squabble: although the Danes were in control of the town itself, the Lübeckers had occupied Krogen, the very castle that was supposed to defend it.

However, a Danish admiral, Peder Skram, employed unexpectedly bold tactics. His fleet had become immobilized because the sea had frozen over, but instead of resigning himself to his fate he gave orders to have the cannon hauled out of his ships and dragged across the ice towards the castle. The Lübeckers were understandably startled by the sight of these guns moving slowly towards them on the ice (an eerie maritime version of Birnam Wood advancing on Dunsinane) and when they saw them all being lined up and aimed menacingly at themselves they decided to capitulate. They were driven out and never came back.

Frederik II, King of
Denmark and Norway.
Engraving by Henrik
Goltzius, 1589.

FRIDERICVS. II. D. G. DANIÆ. NORVEGIE.
&Cˊ. REX.

A trial of strength

Elsinore's fortunes changed in 1559 with the accession to the throne of
Frederik II, aged twenty-five. He was young and ambitious and enter-
tained imperialistic ideas about reconquering Sweden and restoring the
Nordic Union. But it was an unfortunate moment to choose, for the
King of Sweden at the time, Erik XIV, was equally young and equal-
ly ambitious.

One serious bone of contention was a heraldic detail, the 'three
crowns' device in the Swedish royal coat of arms. This had originally
been used to symbolize the Kalmar Union under Margrete, but when
the union was dissolved it continued to be used by the Swedish King
to symbolize Sweden only. Its introduction by the Danish King into his

coat of arms – indicating that he planned to restore the Scandinavian union under his own rule – was understandably regarded by the Swedes as a deliberate provocation. Frederik II decided to settle matters once and for all and declared war. Like so many others, it was intended to be a quick war, for each wanted to teach the other a lesson. But it dragged on for seven years with a total lack of mercy on both sides. Erik XIV's order of the day before one terrible massacre was: "Take no Dane prisoner, but slay everybody and everything as God's grace permits."

The real aim of the war was a trial of strength to determine who was really the ruler of the Baltic, but by the time it was over neither party could claim to be the victor. However, although failing to vanquish Sweden, Denmark demonstrated its naval power and command of the entrance to and exit from the Sound.

Like all wars, it was also a severe drain on Denmark's finances. By 1566 the situation was so serious that Frederik II and his councillors decided as a last resort to enlist the help of a man with special talents named Peder Oxe.

Oxe had actually fled from Denmark in disgrace many years earlier in connection with accusations of criminal financial dealings. But Frederik decided to disregard the old dispute and recall him. Oxe was still acknowledged to be a financial wizard – which was just what Frederik needed.

Erik of Pomerania's toll fee of one English noble per ship had long been regarded by skippers and shipowners as grossly unfair – after all, ships were of so many different sizes, carried so many different cargoes, and, according to nationality, had various interests and affiliations. But the system had also been proving increasingly disadvantageous from the Danish king's point of view. The first four or five kings after Erik of Pomerania had therefore continually tried to introduce amendments of one kind or another, and these in turn made it necessary to introduce various special concessions. Some nationalities were exempted completely and others enjoyed preferential treatment in certain respects.

There were some curious rules. For a long time any ship carrying salt, regardless of nationality, had to hand over six barrels – and also one-thirtieth of all the wine it carried.

Ships of all nations also had to pay clerkage fees to cover paperwork and lighthouse fees, which were supposed to compensate in some measure for the expenses involved in supplying fuel to keep flares burning and paying lighthouse keepers to tend them.

Radical reforms

By this time the basic toll had admittedly been raised from one to three nobles per ship, but it was still far from being a satisfactory system.

Peder Oxe realized that the only answer lay in a radical reform of the whole basis upon which the Sound Dues were calculated. Henceforth, instead of a simple toll per ship, payment must be made, he suggested, on the basis of the cargo carried: to start with, two rix-dollars 'per last'.* Soon this was changed to an even subtler and more flexible system: a percentage of the value of each last of cargo. The details of such percentages were moreover kept secret and could always be adjusted.

The King held the right of pre-emption, that is to say an option to buy, if he so chose, all cargoes declared. This royal prerogative encouraged the captain of a ship to make a correct declaration. Naturally, if he thought the King might be interested in buying his cargo, he was tempted to put a high value on it. However, in doing so he ran the risk that His Majesty might be totally disinterested, in which case he would have to pay a duty calculated on this high valuation. Conversely, if he played safe and declared a low value in the hope of getting away with paying a low duty, the King might decide to buy the whole consignment – which could leave the captain seriously out of pocket.

All in all, it was a cunningly double-edged system, and the Danish King was delighted, though it hardly served to increase his popularity among seafaring nations. As an English mariner, Thomas North, wrote to Sir Francis Walsingham in 1582: "The customs which [the Danish King] hath raised of late enrich him very much and cause him to be very quarrelsome with other princes."

Customs officers were authorized to buy not only luxury goods for the royal table and household on the King's behalf but virtually any kind of merchandise: roofing tiles, tar, hemp – even elephant tusks and parrots.

Skippers were not the only ones tempted to make false declarations. Customs officers themselves were sometimes willing to turn a blind eye in return for a a share of the profit; deals could be made on the side, but as long as they went undetected only the King stood to lose.

* A last was a term used at the time to denote a certain weight, capacity or quantity, varying according to the nature of the merchandise. In terms of weight it represented about 2 tons; a last of herring could be about 12 barrels, and as a measure of grain or malt it might represent about 80 bushels. An additional sly touch was the imposition of half a rix-dollar for every last of ballast.

Ships that tried to slip through the Great Belt or the Little Belt might find themselves challenged and attacked by Danish patrol boats. Those who protested against valuations of their cargoes or the dues imposed ran the risk of having them raised out of hand "just to teach them a lesson".

Every ship, regardless of nationality, was obliged to dip its flag and strike its topsails when passing Elsinore. Any vessel that failed to do so was regarded as 'hostile' and a cannon-ball would be sent flying across its bows as a warning. When the captain then cast anchor and had himself rowed ashore to pay his Sound Dues, he might well find himself presented with a bill for the cost of the shot. Even the Danish King himself never sailed past the fortress without displaying the same symbolic courtesy to his own power.

On one occasion an English ambassador visiting Denmark high-handedly refused to let the captain of his ship strike his topsails, insisting that as Queen Elizabeth's official emissary he was exempt from such a subservient gesture. It was unwise of him: the castle guns roared and two of his sailors were killed.

The number of ships passing through the Sound and calling at Elsinore to pay toll increased steadily. Prior to 1500 the figure was about 1,000 annually, but towards the end of the sixteenth century it had risen to well over 5,000. Most of them were Dutch. Baltic trade was booming; shipowners could well afford to pay the dues demanded by the Danish King.

A more resplendent fortress

Summoning Peder Oxe to reorganize the levying of the Sound Dues proved to be a masterful stroke: within a few years the King's income from this source practically tripled.

By 1570 Frederik had brought the war with Sweden to an end without achieving his objective – the situation was virtually a stalemate. Two years later, at the age of thirty-eight, he married his fifteen-year-old cousin, Sophie of Mecklenburg, and in 1574 embarked upon what was to become the major architectural project of his life: the building of a new castle at Elsinore.

Erik of Pomerania's old fortress was quite imposing. Its position was still uniquely dramatic, and by converting it into a sumptuous modern residence it would continue to demonstrate to the world the power and affluence of the Danish monarch. New defensive bastions had been added at all four corners between 1558 and 1560, just before Frederik came to the throne. But he also needed to increase the castle's striking power, and therefore gave orders for a big, strong, square gun tower to be built. Today it looks rather like a fifteenth-century donjon (for which it is sometimes mistaken) but originally it had a spire to match the others.

The old castle's rooms were cold and gloomy, by no means adequately comfortable and luxurious for his new young Queen – let alone for receiving and entertaining diplomats and ambassadors from abroad.

At first Frederik's intention was merely to modernize the medieval fortress, but in the end he built a completely new palace on top of the old square curtain wall, most of which was encased within new walls of red brick decorated with horizontal bands of sandstone. Doorways and windows had decorative sandstone architraves, the roof was covered with red tiles and everything was executed in what became known in Northern Europe as the Dutch Renaissance style.

As a maritime nation, Denmark had always had considerable contact with the Netherlands, where at this time general unrest as a result of the Protestant uprising (and vicious attempts to suppress it by Philip II of Spain) made it extremely difficult for the country's many gifted artists and artisans to find work. Many of them therefore emigrated, especially to Northern Germany and Denmark, where the political situation was more stable and rich patrons had plenty of money to spend.

Frederik's new castle evolved haphazardly. There was never any initial, comprehensive plan, and such plans covering one phase or another as were made from time to time were often changed – regardless of expense. The whole project took about eleven years to complete, during which period two different architects were engaged on it.

The first was Hans van Paeschen, a Dutch specialist in fortifications who had been in Frederik II's service ever since 1564 and moreover was a skilled sculptor with a thorough grounding in Italian architecture.

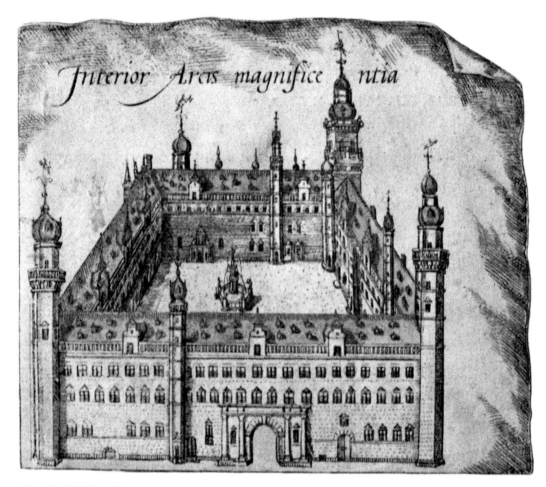

Detail of the Braunius
engraving on pp.58–59.
Frederik II wanted a
magnificent castle with
many towers and spires.

But after a while Frederik wearied of him and replaced him with a much younger man, Antonis van Opbergen, also a Dutchman. Frederik also had many ideas of his own, not all of which coincided at any time with those of his architect. It was all a process of more or less inspired improvisation.

Most of the building materials had to be imported. Timber came from Norway, marble and a hard type of sandstone from Halland, one of the Danish provinces in what is now southern Sweden and a softer kind of sandstone suitable for fireplaces, newel staircases and various forms of ornamentation from the island of Gotland. 600,000 to 800,000 bricks and roofing tiles were ordered from Emden in Holland – simply because the quality was said to be superior to that obtainable in Denmark.

The Ballroom at
Elsinore Castle as
it looks today.

The first phase, 1574–79, was under the direction of van Paeschen, who created a strongly fortified and sumptously appointed palace with a huge ballroom, a magnificent chapel royal and a whole new south wing to enable the Queen and her ladies-in-waiting to walk to and from all parts of the building without getting their feet wet.

So much had been achieved by 1577 that Frederik decided it was time to give his new castle a more dignified name. Henceforth it was to be known as Kronborg (Crown Castle) and he issued a decree to the effect that anybody heard using the old name, Krogen, was to be fined "one fat ox". As fines go it was rather severe – just for forgetting oneself in conversation – but there is no record of its ever actually having been imposed.

Frederik paused for a while in 1579, but then conceived some new and even more extravagant ideas. To start with, he felt that the castle's whole appearance, now that it was completed and he could see it, was too dull, not nearly resplendent enough. So he instructed a painter to give the south wing a coat of white lead and linseed oil to see what the effect would be. Apparently it pleased him, for he then instructed his

Queen Sophie, Frederik II's consort.

architect to have all the walls completely covered with slabs of pale sandstone. Once again, these had to be quarried in Halland and brought across to Elsinore.

Next, there was trouble with the roofs. Severe winters had taken their toll, and in some places snow and ice had penetrated to the roof‑ing timbers, after which rot had set in. Frederik therefore gave orders for all the expensive, high quality tiles he had imported from Emden to be ripped off again: the roofs and spires were now to be covered with sheet copper instead.

With the passing of time, these expanses of copper naturally acquired a layer of pale green verdigris. But how brightly they must have shone when they were new! The description of the castle in the Braunius & Hohenbergius atlas – "a beautiful building whose roofs and spires glow in the sunshine like gold" – becomes more understandable.

The Elsinore tapestries

The new roof was by no means the end to Frederik's extravagances. A year or two previously he had placed two commissions for works of art that were to become renowned throughout Europe.

The first was for a series of tapestries to decorate his huge new ballroom. Tapestries not only gratified the period's demands for decorative magnificence but also had the advantage of rendering a room's acoustics more agreeable and – especially in the north of Europe – of making it easier to heat.

Frederik II gave this commission to a Flemish tapestry-weaver named Hans Knieper, who was already his court painter. Knieper was instructed to set up a manufactory at Elsinore, buy whatever materials he needed in Antwerp, engage as many Flemish weavers as he liked and bring them to Denmark with their families. He painted all the cartoons himself and personally supervised the entire weaving process. At one period he had twenty looms going at the same time; the work was completed between 1581 and 1585.

Frederik's ballroom was so big that an exceptionally large number of tapestries was needed. They had to be made to fit the wall spaces between the windows on both sides of the long hall. The agreed price for the whole series was 9,000 rix-dollars.* Frederik also commissioned a magnificent canopy to be erected over his table at one end of the hall whenever he gave a banquet. It was in three sections, woven splendidly in gold and silver thread as well as red and purple silks; these three extra pieces alone cost him an additional 2,000 rix-dollars.

What made Frederik II's tapestries exceptional was not merely their number but also their subject matter: he wished all the kings of Denmark to be portrayed against backgrounds of stately buildings and luxuriant scenery with accompanying German translations of Danish verses (both languages were spoken in the kingdom) describing their respective achievements.

In the normal way, the most popular subjects depicted on series of tapestries at the time were scenes from the Bible or ancient Greek mythology. However, genealogical series were often favoured by European monarchs during the sixteenth century; the Scandinavians in particular had displayed a strong interest in tracing the history of their forbears and kings as far back as possible, their aim being to establish their dignity as being in no way inferior to the royal houses of Mediterranean Europe.

* By comparison, Frederik II paid Knieper a retainer of 100 rix-dollars a year. Frederik's son, Christian IV, paid England's famous composer and lutenist John Dowland what was regarded at the time as the unusually handsome annual salary of 500 rix-dollars.

Erik of Pomerania after losing his crown.
Detail of tapestry by Hans Knieper.

Frederik's wish to have all the kings of Denmark portrayed proved to be a very tall order indeed, for a twelfth-century Danish historian, Saxo Grammaticus, had written a history of Denmark, *Gesta Danorum*, in which he claimed to have traced an impressive total of 111 kings, the first being Dan, a contemporary of King David of the Old Testament.* Saxo's history, written in Latin (and widely known from manuscript copies in the late Middle Ages) was not actually published until 1514. Some of it was acknowledged to be legendary in character. Frederik's own court historiographer, Anders Sørensen Vedel, who himself had published a translation into Danish of Saxo's history in 1575, was especially sceptical, with the result that, on Vedel's advice, the number of kings to be included in the tapestry series was reduced to 100, including Frederik himself and his son, later Christian IV. An inventory has been preserved which indicates that originally there were 43 tapestries, including the canopy. Some of them depicted two, three, four and even six kings; most of the figures were about two metres high including helmet or crown.

Vedel's scepticism about Saxo's long list of Danish kings resulted in three notable (and in the eyes of posterity regrettable) omissions in the Elsinore tapestries: a king named Horwendil, his brother Fengo, and Horwendil's son Amleth,** namely the three key persons in the legend on which Shakespeare based his tragedy. According to Saxo's chronicle, Fengo had murdered Horwendil and seized both his throne and his wife, Gerutha, whereupon Amleth, afraid of what his evil uncle might think of doing next, feigned madness, which gave him a chance to avenge his father's death by a clever ruse.

In Saxo's history of Denmark (Books 1 to 16) half of Book 3 and most of Book 4 are devoted to the Hamlet legend. Why then did Frederik II's court historiographer reject these kings so emphatically? The reason was probably ideological rather than historical: Saxo portrayed Amleth as a rebel, a would-be usurper, and therefore unworthy to be represented in Frederik's genealogical tree.

Most of the tapestries were about four metres high and three metres wide. A mark woven into them – a crown symbol and the letter B – is a rebus meaning Kronborg. This could have been Knieper's private whim. According to a statute issued in the Netherlands in 1528, all tapestries manufactured in Brussels had to have a woven mark, a shield between two Bs, signifying Brussels in Brabant. Having woven all his

---

* A Swedish historian, Johannes Magnus, nettled by this Danish claim, published in 1544 a history of Sweden in which he proudly outshone Saxo by listing a total of no less than 143 Swedish kings, claiming that the first of these was Noah's son Japheth, who had managed to survive the Flood around 2500 BC. Erik XIV of Sweden was so delighted with this revelation that he promptly commissioned a series of tapestries depicting 'all the kings of Sweden'. Only four were ever completed, but it was probably Erik XIV's initiative that prompted Frederik II to go one better.

** The anglicized spelling of the Danish Amled, in which the final 'd' is pronounced softly, as in 'with'. The Danish name is derived from the Old Norse *amlode*, meaning a simpleton.

Frederik II and
his son Christian
(later Christian IV).
Tapestry executed
by Hans Knieper.

Weaver's mark on
Elsinore tapestries,
a rebus interpreted
as Kronborg
(Crown Castle)

Kronborg tapestries at Elsinore, Knieper presumably felt that a crown and at least one B would be an elegant variation.

Only fourteen of these tapestries have been preserved in Denmark: seven are still in Elsinore Castle and seven are in the National Museum in Copenhagen. The three-piece table canopy was seized as war booty by the Swedes in 1659.

The King's fountain

Frederik's second highly extravagant artistic commission went to Georg Labenwolf, a renowned German bronze founder in Nuremberg, who was instructed to make a magnificent fountain to be erected in the castle's inner courtyard.

It was to consist of a hexagonal stone basin, a central column in four tiers like a wedding-cake, and about thirty-six bronze statues, which were to be executed by the Dutch sculptor Gregorius van der Schardt. These figures were to include Juno, Minerva, Venus and Diana, sundry genii, dolphins and sirens, archers and harquebusiers of various European and Oriental nationalities, and at the very top, Neptune himself, clasping his trident, standing in a conch-shell and driving his team of sea-horses. The whole fanciful construction was about seven metres high.

By means of an intricate system of copper pipes, jets of water were to spew in all directions from the jaws of the mythical creatures, the nostrils of the dolphins, the tips of the arrows, the muzzles of the muskets, the breasts of the goddesses, the prongs of the trident and also from as many other suitable orifices as possible.

The power harnessed to make this extraordinary fountain play was gravity. There was a hill to the southwest of Elsinore, only a kilometre or so from the castle, the top of which was on a level with the castle's spires. By establishing a conduit system from streams and dams on this hill all the way down to the fountain in the castle courtyard, sufficient water pressure was obtained not only to make all the jets of water spew as required but also, as a particularly novel feature, to keep the figure of Neptune and his seahorses continually revolving.

All these complicated refinements took time, and Frederik's patience was sorely tried. Although he had signed the contract with Labenwolf in 1576, eight years were to pass before the fountain was finally inaugurated in 1584. But by then it was indeed a wonder to behold.

Frederik II's elaborate fountain, designed by Gregorius van der Schardt, originally stood in the centre of the courtyard at Elsinore Castle. After a drawing c. 1583 by W.J. von Stromer.

A whole volley of shot

By the time Frederik II had finished building his new castle its fame had already spread and its praises were highly sung, for it was acknowledged to be not only an architectural achievement unparalleled in Europe in terms of magnificence, strength and uniqueness of position, but also a dynamic symbol of the power of the Danish monarch, his command of the Baltic and above all his ability to compel the maritime nations of the world to continue paying large sums of money directly into his coffers.

Frederik II repeatedly boasted that the building of Kronborg had never imposed any burden on the nation, which in a sense was true: all expenses, including the spectacular series of tapestries and the fantastic fountain, had been met by the income obtained from the Sound Dues, which was under his personal control.

One of Frederik II's first opportunities to draw full-scale attention to the splendours of his new royal seat was in 1582, when Queen Elizabeth of England graciously let it be known that she wished to honour the King of Denmark by investing him with the Order of the Garter, her ulterior motive being to strengthen England's ties with Denmark and secure Denmark's support against Philip II of Spain.

Frederik was highly flattered and promptly requested Elizabeth to instruct her emissaries to bring the insignia of the order, not to Copenhagen, his capital, but to Kronborg Castle at Elsinore. Elizabeth duly sent Lord Willoughby of Eresby, accompanied by a large retinue. Accounts of the visit were widely circulated. In his subsequent report, Willoughby said the Danish King had entertained them "most royally". He also mentioned that during a splendid banquet, the Danish King, after making "affectionate and loving speeches" to Elizabeth, had done him the great honour of causing "a whole volley of shot" to be fired by the guns of the fortress, testifying to the world at large that England and Denmark were on the most amicable of terms.

It is an interesting detail, for no previous record exists in Denmark of an ambassador ever having being honoured in this way. Shakespeare was only eighteen at the time and still in Stratford, but it must have come to his ears in some way, for he used it in *Hamlet* as a historically accurate touch of local colour that might well have been appreciated by some of the better-informed members of Elizabethan audiences. At the very end of the play, Hamlet hears "a march afar off and shot within" and asks:

> What warlike noise is this?   (V.ii.356)

and Osric answers:

> Young Fortinbras, with conquest come from Poland
> To the ambassadors of England gives
> This warlike volley.

A Danish Queen of England

A few years later the magnificence of Elsinore Castle was once more impressed upon Elizabethan England. As Elizabeth I's long and illustrious reign drew towards its close it became obvious that in all probability she would be succeeded by James VI of Scotland, who had married a Danish princess, Frederik II's daughter Anna, sister of the new young Danish King, Christian IV. The marriage ceremony had first been performed at Kronborg Castle in 1589. James was not present, but had sent a representative – as was the custom – in this case Lord Keith, who duly sat on the ceremonial bridal bed together with Princess Anna.

Anna was anxious to join her real husband. She set forth on a voyage to Scotland with an escort of fourteen warships, but a terrible storm forced the fleet to seek shelter along the Norwegian coast. Subsequent investigations revealed that the fury of the waves must have been deliberately caused by witches, who had apparently sent some devils after the ships in an empty beer barrel. There was simply no doubt about it, for it was common knowledge that winds could be bought and sold like any other service or favour. As a penalty for this terrible deed, a number of women in both Scotland and Denmark were accused and burnt at the stake.

Witches raising a
storm in order to wreck
a ship. Woodcut in
Olaus Magnus,
*Historia de gentibvs
septentrionalibvs* (1555),
Book 3, Chapter 15.

1:1

Disturbed by these events, James set out from Scotland to meet his bride half way. They were united in Oslo, where a marriage ceremony was performed for the second time. In the meantime the bridal couple had received an invitation to visit the Danish court at Elsinore, so they left, just after Christmas, travelling all the way down the western coast of the Scandinavian peninsula. When they reached Helsingborg (the town on the other side of the straits, opposite Elsinore) they found the sea had frozen over, so they were able to drive across the ice without even getting out of their coaches. Accounts of this bold journey as well as other extraordinary tales of travelling and even fighting on frozen Baltic waters were naturally received with amazement in warmer countries unused to such extreme conditions. Shakespeare must have heard some of these stories, for there are several references to the coldness of the climate in *Hamlet*, including Horatio's observation to Marcellus that the frown on the Ghost's face was the same as when Hamlet's father "smote the sledded Polacks on the ice".

James then insisted on having the wedding ceremony performed for the third time. As on the first occasion, it was conducted in the Great Hall at Kronborg Castle – Queen Sophie's ballroom. It was one of the many festive occasions on which Frederik's new tapestries were brought out and hung on the walls.

As the fame of these tapestries had already spread through Europe it gave Shakespeare an opportunity to incorporate yet another authentic detail in *Hamlet*. He had already used the device of a loose wall-hanging or arras (so named after the French town of Arras in Artois, renowned for its tapestry manufacture) as a hiding-place for a person

James VI of Scotland
(James I of England)
and his consort, Frederik
II's daughter, Princess
Anna, sister of Christian
IV (Anne of Denmark).
Artist unknown.

on stage in *King John* (1596), when Hubert hides the two villains who were to put out Arthur's eyes (IV.i.2) and again in *The Merry Wives of Windsor* (written about the same time as *Hamlet*) for Falstaff to hide behind in Ford's house (III.iii.96). So one of the sumptuous tapestries in the Danish King's castle was eminently suitable for Polonius to hide behind.

Frederik II revelled in his power quite ostentatiously. On one occasion he gave orders to have all ships detained at Elsinore for a fort-night, merely to give himself the pleasure of entertaining a visitor from abroad with an extraordinary sight from the windows of the castle at the end of this period: over seven hundred ships, all, with his royal permission, weighing anchor, setting sail and leaving at the same time.

Frederik died in 1588. The priest who officiated at his funeral declared that "had his Majesty drunk a little less he might have lived a little longer". He was succeeded by his son, Christian IV, who was only eleven and therefore kept under the guidance of a regency until his coronation in 1596. The event was celebrated with a display of extravagance that would have pleased his father. After three weeks of festivity in Copenhagen, the whole court moved to Elsinore for the grand finale, where the last three days were spent in a riot of feasting, pageants and tournaments, culminating with a mock battle in the course of which a staggering total of 86,000 fireworks were let off.

Christian IV was naturally pleased with his inheritance, especially the knowledge that whenever he needed money he could always dip into his income from the Sound Dues. He frequently declared that he regarded the Sound as the most brilliant of all the jewels in his crown and one of the most important regalias that God and nature had given to his kingdom.

Shakespeare could be quite sure that Elizabethan audiences would have heard about the Danish castle at Elsinore.

A wineglass used by Frederik II at a banquet in 1568. He and many of his guests scratched their names on it, after which it was preserved as a memento, now in the Rosenborg Collection, Copenhagen. Height: 40 cm.

PART TWO

A question left us yet to prove

Was Shakespeare's 'Elsinore' just based on hearsay?

It has long been recognized that Shakespeare went to greater lengths to introduce local colour into the plays he set in a foreign country than any of his contemporaries. He is also the only Elizabethan playwright to have made such a serious attempt to create a specifically Danish background. Just as the accuracy of the touches of local colour in some of the scenes in the Italian plays – for example in *Romeo and Juliet* and *The Merchant of Venice*, but especially the Venetian atmosphere in the first act of *Othello* and the Paduan background in *The Taming of the Shrew* – has caused many people to believe that he must have witnessed these details himself, the knowledge of Danish customs and conditions Shakespeare displays in *Hamlet* has prompted some commentators to believe that he must also have visited Elsinore at some time.

In the case of *Hamlet*, many divergent views have been expressed. Some scholars have gone so far as to dismiss the significance of 'Denmark' and 'Elsinore' completely. A Danish translator of the complete works has contended that "the circumstances and characters presented in *Hamlet* are not Danish: the train of thought is English and the interests confined to London" (Valdemar Østerberg, 1920); a renowned English Shakespearean scholar once wrote even more categorically that "Hamlet is an English prince, the court of Elsinore is modelled upon the English court, and the Danish constitution that of England under the Virgin Queen" (J. Dover Wilson, 1935); and a modern Danish translator has chimed in, declaring that "the play does not take place in any exact geographical location, its 'Elsinore' has nothing really to do with Elsinore or Kronborg, and the few references to topographical surroundings bear no relation to North Zealand" (Johannes Sløk, 1971).

Cashbook entries covering wages paid to English actors in 1585, including William Kempe (Wilhelm Kempe), George Bryan (Jurgen Briann) and Thomas Pope.

Despite these sweeping scholarly claims, the text of the play still provides much evidence that Shakespeare took considerable trouble to create a Danish background that would at least sound convincing to Elizabethan audiences. The geographical setting of the play is established in the very first scene by references to Denmark, Norway and Poland. Shakespeare then makes it abundantly clear that the setting is the royal castle at Elsinore, that Elsinore is a port, that the King of Denmark is in residence with his court, that the castle has the customary battlements, guns and a platform* where sentinels keep watch, and also a chapel. The terms 'Denmark' and 'Dane' appear continually, in all about 30 times.

Throughout the play there are explicit references in both stage directions and the dialogue to the roaring of guns, rolling of drums and 'braying' of trumpets that formed such an integral part of Danish court life at the time, especially in connection with roisterous drinking customs.

It has been claimed that just because Shakespeare introduced local colour of this kind it is no proof that he ever visited Denmark, for he could easily have gathered information about Elsinore and the extravagances of the Danish court from other sources, including all kinds

* **platform** a level place for mounting guns in a battery. Shakespeare uses the word in the same sense in *Othello* II.iii.126 ('A hall in the castle'): "To the platform, masters; come, let's set the watch."

Page from the 1623 Folio edition of Shakespeare's works edited by Heminge and Condell. William Kempe (Kempt), Thomas Pope (Poope) and George Bryan were in the troupe of actors that performed before Frederik II at Elsinore Castle in 1585.

The Workes of William Shakespeare, containing all his Comedies, Histories, and Tragedies: Truely set forth, according to their first ORIGINALL.

The Names of the Principall Actors in all these Playes.

William Shakespeare.
Richard Burbadge.
John Hemmings.
Augustine Phillips.
William Kempt.
Thomas Poope.
George Bryan.
Henry Condell.
William Slye.
Richard Cowly.
John Lowine.
Samuell Crosse.
Alexander Cooke.

Samuel Gilburne.
Robert Armin.
William Ostler.
Nathan Field.
John Underwood.
Nicholas Tooley.
William Ecclestone.
Joseph Taylor.
Robert Benfield.
Robert Goughe.
Richard Robinson.
Iohn Shancke.
Iohn Rice.

of hearsay provided by merchants, sailors, travelling journeymen, members of diplomatic missions and – perhaps in particular – English fellow-actors, especially William Kempe, Thomas Pope and George Bryan, who are known to have belonged to a troupe employed at the Danish court in 1585–86 and subsequently became members of Shakespeare's own company, the Chamberlain's Men.

It has also been suggested that Shakespeare could have gleaned information from English musicians who had visited Denmark, especially from John Dowland, the lutenist and song-writer who was retained at the Danish court on an annual basis between 1598 and 1606.

A cashbook entry in Elsinore's municipal accounts for 1586/87 records an outlay of *4 skilling* for repairing a board fence which was "torn down by people when the English acted in the Town Hall court-yard".

However, there is another school of thought. Some commentators have found it hard to believe that so many of the little touches in the play that are either accurately Danish – or meant to be Danish – could have been pieced together just from books, maps or casual conversation. The view has been expressed that a discernible difference exists between the kind of straightforward fact which some of Shakespeare's informants might have thought worth relating over a glass of wine in a Bankside tavern and certain details, perhaps at first sight insignificant, which Shakespeare would surely only have noted if he had either observed them himself, or heard them mentioned while in Denmark. It has been suggested that vivid, descriptive writing can only stem from such personal experience, not from information received at second or third hand.

Supporters of this school of thought have therefore drawn attention to what they term "the weight of circumstantial evidence". One has declared that "there is every probability that [Shakespeare] visited Elsinore and made use of what he heard and saw there" (Laurits Pedersen, 1916), and another that "there is a likelihood so strong it almost amounts to certainty. Every time I return to the subject [it] seems stronger than before and an inner voice tells me: Of course he was here!" (Julius Clausen, 1924). In recent years the door has been kept ajar by a Danish historian who refers to "the Elsinore William Shakespeare himself had visited, or had heard about from good compatriots who had frequented Elsinore" (Kenno Pedersen, 1996).

Title page of John
Dowland's *The Second
Booke of Songs or Ayres*,
dedicated to Lucy,
Countess of Bedford.

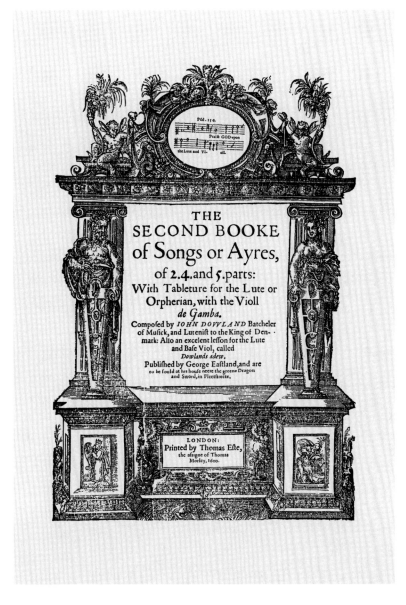

*I moſt humbly beſeech your La : to receiue this worke, into your fauour: and
the rather, becauſe it commeth far to beg it, of you. From Helſingnoure
in Denmarke the firſt of Iune.*

1600.

Elsinore Castle in the winter of 2000. Apart from the missing spire on the square cannon tower (see p. 32) it must have looked very much the same in the winter of 1600.

'Tis bitter cold

In the Ghost scenes on the platform of the Castle at the beginning of the play, Shakespeare indicates how miserably cold it is. First, Francisco gives Barnardo "much thanks" for relieving him from his spell of sentry duty because "'Tis bitter cold" (I.i.8), and when Horatio and Marcellus appear and are challenged with a "Say, what, is Horatio there?" Horatio answers "A piece of him", which is interpreted by some commentators as a humourous indication that the hand he holds out is all that is left of him – the rest is shrivelled up with cold.

Nor does Shakespeare leave it at that. The moment Hamlet comes onto the platform of the battlements to see if the Ghost will appear again he says:

> The air bites shrewdly, it is very cold.   (I.iv.1)

and Horatio quickly agrees:

It is a nipping and an eager air.

There seems to be no particular reason for this repeated stressing of how cold it was, for it has no bearing on the frightening apparition of Hamlet's father's Ghost and the terrible story he wants to tell Hamlet. So could it be that Shakespeare, having personally experienced this bitter cold, could never forget it and was unable to resist the urge to emphasize it?

For, as some commentators have observed, can it really be mere coincidence that the eastern parapet is notoriously the coldest, most windswept spot in the whole Castle?

The bell then beating one

In connection with the Ghost's appearance and disappearance, a com-
plication arises with the curiously rapid passing of the hours between
midnight and dawn. The time of night is established very clearly when
the play opens. Francisco observes:

> You come most carefully upon your hour.
>
> (I.i.6)

and Barnardo answers:

> 'Tis now struck twelve.

and again in Barnardo's description of what had happened the night
before

> Last night of all, ...
>
> ...
>
> The bell then beating one ...   (I.i.38–42)

Shakespeare also makes it quite clear that it is not only a cold night
but also an ominously dark and silent one:

> Thus twice before and jump*at this dead hour
>
> (I.i.67)

But suddenly a cock crows, and off stalks the Ghost, apparently at
this signal. What makes a cock crow in the middle of the night? Shakespeare knew his audiences would expect an explanation – and he did
not disappoint them:

> It faded on the crowing of the cock.
> Some say that ever 'gainst** that season comes
> Wherein our Saviour's birth is celebrated,
> This bird of dawning singeth all night long;
>
> (I.i.162–65)

But hardly has this matter been clarified when Horatio observes:

> So have I heard ...
> But look, the morn in russet mantle clad
> Walks o'er the dew of yon high eastward hill
>
> (I.i.170–72)

*   **jump** precisely
** **'gainst** in anticipation of

One thing is a cock 'crowing for Christmas' in the middle of the night to ward off evil spirits, but how could the sun manage to rise in midwinter so soon after the clock has struck one?

Those in the 'Shakespeare-was-here' school see this as an indication that he must have visited Elsinore in the late spring or early summer and experienced the extraordinary shortness and beauty of a Nordic night, when the "morn, in russet mantle clad" really does begin to glow in the sky at 2 or 3 o'clock.

As a Swedish commentator has put it, just as it may be difficult for an Englishman to imagine a sea coast without the ebb and flow of a tide, "it is almost impossible for anyone to imagine the enchantment of a Nordic summer's night without having experienced it" (Gunnar Sjögren, 1962).

As for the objection that the lines "'Tis bitter cold" and "the air bites shrewdly" must refer to a winter situation, any Scandinavian knows that in the early summer the nights can be extremely chilly during the short interval between sunset and sunrise. It has also been observed that the flowers enumerated by Ophelia – columbines, daisies and "coronet weeds" – were the field-flowers of the late spring, and that this was surely the season Shakespeare intended to convey.

But then what about the reference to "our Saviour's birth" – irrefutably Christmas? Why should Shakespeare transfer a magical, possibly early summertime experience into a scene set in mid-winter?

Could it just be poetic licence? After all, this instance in *Hamlet* was neither the first nor the last. In *Richard III* (1592–93), after a number of ghosts have appeared to the King in his dreams on Bosworth Field, he suddenly starts up and says:

> Soft, I did but dream ...
> ... It is now dead midnight   (V.iii.178–80)

but only twenty-seven lines later, at the end of his soliloquy, in comes Ratcliffe and says blandly:

> The early village-cock
> Hath twice done salutation to the morn:

There is a similar scene in *Othello* (1604). Othello and Desdemona retire to their sheets, bidding Cassio and Iago an early goodnight. Iago notes (II.iii.12): "'tis not yet ten o' the clock". However, after a drinking bout and some roistering and scuffling, Iago suddenly announces :

> By the mass, 'tis morning
> Pleasure and action make the hours seem short.
>
> (II.iii.384-85)

Could Shakespeare have taken a similar liberty in *Hamlet*?

Yon high eastward hill

Horatio's observation about the dawn includes a reference to "yon high eastward hill". Commentators in the dismissive school have been quick to pounce on this as clear proof that Shakespeare can never have visited Elsinore, for had he done so, surely he would never have made this 'famous error'? They point out that there is nothing even faintly resembling a hill on the Swedish coast directly east of Elsinore.

But supporters of the 'Shakespeare-was-here' school are not so easily deterred. They contend that even if the Swedish coastline immediately to the east boasts of no more than a long, low-lying ridge, about 40 metres above sea level, there most certainly is a pronounced hill, all of 188 metres high, on the other side of the water, some 28 kilometres north of Elsinore, on Cape Kullen. Already at this time it was moreover a navigation landmark well-known to sailors – rough silhouettes of it were even included on a contemporary chart to help recognition.

Seen from Elsinore, this little hill is relatively insignificant and would therefore hardly be the sort of detail Shakespeare's informants would have bothered to draw his attention to when they came back to England.

On the other hand, if Shakespeare had actually visited the castle at Elsinore himself and stood on "the platform where we keep our watch" he would have been bound to notice it. If he then, with poetic images constantly flitting through his mind, had imagined, or even actually seen the dawn rising, surely he would not have let himself be worried by the fact that this convenient elevation did not strictly lie to the east of Kronborg Castle?

Sceptics point out, however, that he might also have seen an etching of the castle in an atlas published towards the end of the sixteenth cen-

Landfalls of Cape Kullen from the oldest Danish navigation manual, published by Laurentz Benedicht in 1568.

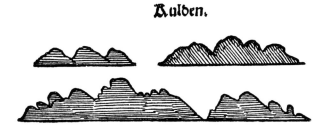

Kulben.

tury by Braunius & Hohenbergius in which a hill named Koll (Cape Kullen) is clearly indicated on the Swedish coast. If so, not only would he have seen that this hill lies far to the north of Kronborg but also surely have spotted the word Oost on the right of the drawing, meaning East. They therefore claim that the only conclusion to be drawn is that he can never have visited Elsinore and never seen this drawing either.

But then what did prompt him to speak of "yon high eastward hill"?

It so happens that another etching exists, dating from 1588, which does in fact show a little hill on the other side of the water. If Shakespeare had seen this etching he could hardly be blamed for not knowing that this hill did not exist in reality and that it can only have been a figment of the artist's imagination that had been added, like a number of other inaccurate features, for purely decorative purposes.

Perhaps it was just a case of one imaginative artist inspiring another?

Such daily cast of brazen cannon

In the very first scene of the play, Shakespeare uses the question-and-answer technique to establish the political tension existing between Norway and Denmark at the time. Marcellus asks four quick questions:

> Why this same strict and most observant watch
> So nightly toils the subject* of the land,
> And why such daily cast of brazen cannon
> And foreign mart for implements of war,
> Why such impress** of shipwrights, whose sore task
> Does not divide the Sunday from the week.
> What might be toward that this sweaty haste
> Doth make the night joint-labourer with the day,
> Who is't that can inform me?   (I.i.73–82)

* **toils the subject** imposes a burden on the country's citizens

** **impress** conscription

Engraving in Braunius, *Theatrum Urbium*, *c.* 1580. The Latin text claims that it is an "accvratiss(ima) delineatio" but there are many inaccuracies, one of them being the pronounced little hill on the other side of the straits, directly east of Elsinore, which does not exist.

It so happens that all Marcellus's questions accurately reflect a historically documented 6-month period of particularly 'sweaty haste'
that had existed in 1575, when Denmark was afraid a French fleet
might try to force its way past Elsinore into the Baltic.

The castle was reinforced with all manner of extra weapons and
defensive measures. Every family in the town had to accept having
soldiers billeted on them. To feed all the extra mouths it was even
decided to set aside the long-established rights of the butchers' guild:
in view of the urgency of the situation, everybody was entitled to
slaughter and sell domestic animals – pigs, cattle, sheep, poultry, whatever. Citizens were enjoined to keep their arms ready and report to the
Town Hall the moment the alarm bell rang. Nobody was allowed to
leave the town at night and every man was expected do a stint as a
sentinel on the battlements and platforms of the castle and keep what
Shakespeare was to call a "strict and most observant watch".

This burden was long remembered by the townsfolk of Elsinore.
But was it the sort of story Shakespeare's fellow actors – Kempe, Bryan
or Pope – would have been likely to pick up during the period they were
employed at the Danish court, and even if they had, would they have
bothered to tell him about it when they became members of his company in 1594? Or was it perhaps more likely something Shakespeare
could have heard about much earlier in the course of conversation with
Danes in Elsinore, when recollections of this terrible period would
have been fresher in people's minds, for example at some time between
1585 and 1592, the so-called 'lost years' in Shakespeare's life about
which virtually nothing is known?

Even the mention of daily casting of *brazen* cannon is carefully
accurate, for whereas English cannon were usually made of iron,
Danish cannon were of brass; there was one foundry in Copenhagen
and another had been established in Elsinore in 1599.

The dreadful summit of the cliff

Another problem is posed by the lines when Horatio expresses his
concern that the Ghost might wish to do Hamlet some harm:

What if it tempt you toward the flood, my lord
Or to the dreadful summit of the cliff
That beetles* o'er his base into the sea,
Which might deprive your sovereignty of reason
And draw you into madness? Think of it,
The very place puts toys of desperation
Without more motive, into every brain
That looks so many fathoms to the sea
And hears it roar beneath.   (I.iv.69–78)

Sceptics point out that there is nothing anywhere near Elsinore bearing the slightest resemblance to a cliff, in fact that the nearest cliff-like topographical feature is on the coast of Zealand about 80 kilometres south of Elsinore.

Other commentators, however, think the word 'cliff' should not be taken too literally and revert to the possibility that Shakespeare may have seen the Braunius & Hohenbergius drawings of the castle on which the ramparts are represented as being as being awesomely high and unscaleable. They suggest that sailors, particularly when passing Elsinore Castle on board a ship, would have regarded the walls of these bastions as extremely 'cliff-like', and that moreover, from the castle itself, anyone standing on the top might easily have felt frightened when looking down "so many fathoms to the sea".

So might Shakespeare perhaps have sailed past aboard a ship? Or could he himself perhaps have stood on the ramparts of the castle and been awed by the waves pounding on the rocks below?

The sceptics retort that the rampart walls of the castle at Elsinore are no more than a mere 14 metres or so high, and that in similar references to cliffs in earlier plays, for example in *Henry VI, Part II* (1590):

As far as I could ken thy chalky cliffs

(III.ii.101)

and in *The Comedy of Errors* (1592):

I looked for the chalky cliffs, but I could
find no whiteness in them   (III.ii.129)

Shakespeare emphasized their chalky whiteness, confirming that his – and Elizabethan audiences' – notion of a cliff was obviously something like the white limestone cliffs at Dover, which are about 100

* **beetles** overhangs

metres high. The height of the Dover cliffs is moreover indicated by the lines in *King Lear* (1605–06) when Edgar, conveying his 'astonish-ment' that Gloucester should have survived his attempt to put an end to his own life, declares:

> Ten masts at each* make not the altitude
> Which thou hast perpendicularly fell
>
> (IV.vi.53–54)

which makes it reasonable to assume that both Shakespeare himself and Elizabethan audiences would think of a mast as being at least ten metres high.

But even when confronted with arguments of this kind, supporters of the 'Shakespeare-was-here' school are still prepared to dismiss them as prosaic, pointing out that Horatio's whole warning was simply phrased poetically and dramatically to imply that the Ghost could well be identified with the Devil, for it was widely believed at the time that the Devil was responsible for luring people to commit suicide.

You shall nose him

It has sometimes been argued that the references made by Shakespeare to the interior of the castle at Elsinore are only rather vague and could therefore virtually apply to any royal palace. We hear of a lobby where Hamlet walks "four hours together" (II.ii.160-161), of the Queen's closet (III.ii.322–33, III.iii.27 and IV.i.35), of its "neighbour room" into which Hamlet lugs the body of Polonius (III.iv.212) and of a chapel to which the King wishes the body to be taken (IV.i.37 and IV.ii.8).

But in one instance Shakespeare adds a significant detail. In the scene where Hamlet is brought before the King and asked what he has done with the body he replies:

> … if indeed you find him not within this month,
> you shall nose him as you go up the stairs into the lobby.
>
> (IV.iii.35–37)

This reference to stairs leading up to the lobby serves no particular purpose – it has no bearing on the action of the plot – but is none the

* at each end to end

Staircase between the North and East Wings of Elsinore Castle leading from the courtyard right up to the Queen's long, narrow gallery. These are the stairs which Hamlet could be referring to in IV.iii.35–37.

less a demonstrably accurate observation. The Castle's famous banqueting hall, the Great Hall, was connected to the royal apartments in the north wing by a long, narrow corridor or anteroom (which at the time would have been called a lobby in English) and was accessible by a stair tower situated between the north and the east wing. These stairs led to the Queen's Gallery and further up to an open, parapeted terrace, and are most likely to have been the ones used by English actors and 'instrumentalists' when engaged to perform – their stage would

Sixteenth-century
birdcage. Woodcut
in Olaus Magnus,
*Historia de gentibvs
septentrionalibvs* (1555),
Book 19, Chapter 42.

1:1

have been at the east end of the Great Hall. Does the accuracy
of Shakespeare's observation indicate that one of his actor colleagues
– William Kempe, Thomas Pope or George Bryan – might have
given him a careful description of the ballroom, the stairs and the
lobby? Would they, however, have had any strong reason for doing so?
Alternatively, it has been suggested that Shakespeare himself might
perhaps have been in the same troupe for a brief period and therefore
able to make his own observations. The fact that his name was not
recorded in the municipal accounts alongside those of the other three
men is no real proof – so claim upholders of the 'Shakespeare-
was-here' contention – for his participation might well have been only
brief – and simply overlooked.

There is another curious detail. In the course of Hamlet's tirade
against his mother he warns her against the risk of exposing his secret:

> Unpeg the basket on the house's top,
> Let the birds fly...
> And break your own neck down.
>
> (III. iv. 195–98)

Could it be mere coincidence that Frederik II had given Queen
Sophie a present of a bird-cage for her gallery in 1585? And again, is it
the sort of detail Kempe, Bryan or Pope would have bothered to tell
Shakespeare about?

There's rue for you

The warders at Kronborg Castle like to tell visitors about a discovery made late in the nineteenth century which might well prove, they suggest, that Shakespeare must have visited Elsinore and also been closely acquainted with the Castle. Apparently a professor of botany happened to notice a little plant growing out of the brickwork of the ramparts which he immediately recognized as one that is extremely rare in Denmark, in fact only having been recorded at two other places. This discovery soon led to the conclusion being drawn (it is not known by whom) that Shakespeare, ever renowned for his familiarity with flowers and plants, must have been inspired by the sight of it to include it among the flowers which Ophelia distributes in the madness scene:

> There's rue for you. And here's some for me. We may call it
> herb of grace a Sundays.   (IV.v.178–79)

It is understandable that the warders of Kronborg enjoy telling this intriguing story, for it has been part of their repertoire for more than a century.* Unfortunately for those who would like to see it as 'proof', the variety called wall rue (*Asplenium ruta muraria*), which is the one observed by the botanist, is not the same as the ordinary rue (*Ruta grave-olens*) referred to by Shakespeare. Moreover, Shakespeare's use – as so

* The botanist in question, H. Mortensen, published his discovery in *Nordøstsjællands Flora*, Copenhagen 1874.

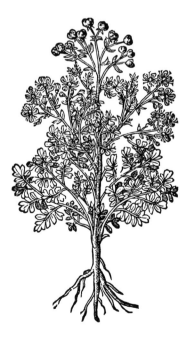

LEFT:
Rue (*Ruta graveolens*) formerly also known as 'herb of grace'. Woodcut, 1648.

RIGHT:
Wall rue (*Ruta muraria*). Woodcut, 1687.

often – is specifically prompted by the opportunity for a pun, rue in the sense of regret, or repentance, which is the very reason why Ophelia offers it symbolically to Claudius, the only one present who has sought to repent.

Besides, Shakespeare had no need to be inspired by a plant he had seen at Elsinore, for he had already used the same wordplay some years earlier in *Richard II*:

> I'll set a bank of rue, sour herb of grace.
>
> (III. iv.105)

To add to the confusion, it is not even known where precisely the nineteenth-century botanist is supposed to have seen the flower growing. Many of the brick-built bastions surrounding the castle date from about 1700, in other words at least a hundred years after Shakespeare's conjectured visit.

Go, get thee to Yaughan

The names of the characters in *Hamlet* would appear to provide virtually nothing to support the theory that Shakespeare might have visited Elsinore. There is, however, one small straw to which believers cling.

Out of a total of eighteen names, only three are clearly Danish: Hamlet, Rosencrantz and Guildenstern; Osric, the name of the foppish character who appears briefly in the last act, sounds slightly Danish but is actually an old Anglo-Saxon name.

Rosencrantz and Guildenstern,* mentioned frequently throughout the play, are the historically correct names of two of the most powerful and influential families of the Danish aristocracy at the time and therefore most aptly chosen for Hamlet's companions. Among the 110 noblemen attending Christian IV's coronation in 1596, nine were Guildensterns and seven were Rosencrantzes, and of the twenty members of the Council permitted to touch the crown before it was placed on the King's head, two were Guildensterns.

A few of the other names in the cast possibly have Danish associations. Gertrude, Hamlet's mother, was a Danish as well as an English

* Spelt 'Gyldenstierne' in Danish and variously in early editions of *Hamlet* as 'Guyldensterne' or 'Gyldersterne'.

name, and Shakespeare may have chosen to use it because, in the Saxo version of the Hamlet legend, Amleth's mother is called Gerutha. He may also have believed that Cornelius was a Danish name (it is actually Dutch). One of the ambassadors sent by the King to Norway, Voltemand (variously spelt Voltimand or Valtemand) could be a corruption of Valdemar, which was the name of several medieval Danish kings. Reynaldo, the servant of Polonius, might possibly be derived from the Danish Regnwald (or Reinolt or Reinholt), but could just as well be a variant of Reynard – a suggestion of the foxiness required of him.

But there is nothing Danish whatsoever about the many Latin and Greek names – Claudius, Polonius, Laertes and all the others – with the result that various reasons, or literary allusions, have been suggested to explain why Shakespeare chose them.

However, one character, though he never makes an appearance, is also quite clearly referred to, and his name is most unusual. At one point the Gravedigger turns to his Companion and says:

> Go, get thee to Yaughan; fetch me a stoup of liquor.
>
> (V.i.60)

This has been called one of the play's 'minor mysteries'. The spelling corresponds to that of the English name Vaughan, perhaps indicating that Shakespeare pronounced it in his mind as one syllable, rhyming with 'yawn',* and that if so he might have been trying to convey the Danish name Jørgen, which is similarly pronounced as one syllable but rhymes more closely with 'yearn'.

On the other hand, most modern Shakespearean editors have decided that Yaughan was Shakespeare's attempt to represent the Danish name Johan, which is pronounced as two syllables (the 'j' as 'y', as in 'yon').

Since Johan corresponds to John, it has also been proposed, rather vaguely, that this could have been a reference to an unidentified innkeeper of this name just round the corner from the Globe Theatre – for the amusement of the groundlings.

However, the possibility of identifying a contemporary Danish innkeeper named Johan (Johannes in full, or Hans for short) some- where within 'stoup-fetching' distance of Kronborg Castle has also been investigated – with intriguing results. There was once an inn called Lundegaard Kro, about halfway between Kronborg Castle and Elsinore, that was particularly well known to the artisans, entertainers

*   This pronunciation is listed by Helge Kökeritz in *Shakespeare's Names. A Pronouncing Dictionary.*

and servants of many kinds employed by the Danish court during the reigns of Frederik II and Christian IV, including Flemish weavers and stonemasons, German blacksmiths and wood-carvers, Italian glass-makers, English musicians and actors, travelling clowns and acrobats from all over Europe, stablemen, coachmen, riding-masters and many more. They would all be accomodated either at the inn or in some big adjoining barns that had been converted into lodging houses, and they would all be sent to the inn for their meals, because the King had found this arrangement cheaper than paying them a daily subsistence allowance. Preserved records reveal that from 1585 until about the turn of the century, three successive innkeepers at Lundegaard Kro were all known as 'Hans'.

There is another curious detail. This inn formed part of an estate called Lundegaard, or Lundehave, a royal country seat set in a beautiful pleasure garden. It had been built by Frederik II between 1586 and 1588 for personal recreational purposes, on the former site of the Franciscan monastery of St Anne, which had been dissolved during the Reformation. He then renamed it Kronborg Have (Kronborg Garden). In the course of drainage work and excavations during the early years of the twentieth century, an unusually large number of human skeletons were dug up. The conclusion drawn – which has not been refuted – is that the Franciscan monastery must obviously have had its own graveyard.

Some commentators have therefore found it tempting to believe that Shakespeare, while staying at the inn together with other English actors, might have come across some gardeners unearthing skulls and bones and later been inspired by the incident to insert his unusual grave-yard scene in *Hamlet*, which contributes nothing to the plot and serves merely as a device for introducing philosophical reflections on life and the inevitability of death before plunging into the play's last and most terrible scene.

But sceptics dismiss the existence of this graveyard, of the inn where so many people in the service of the Danish court – including English actors and 'instrumentalists' – used to have their meals, and of three innkeepers all named Hans, as amounting to no more than pure coincidence.

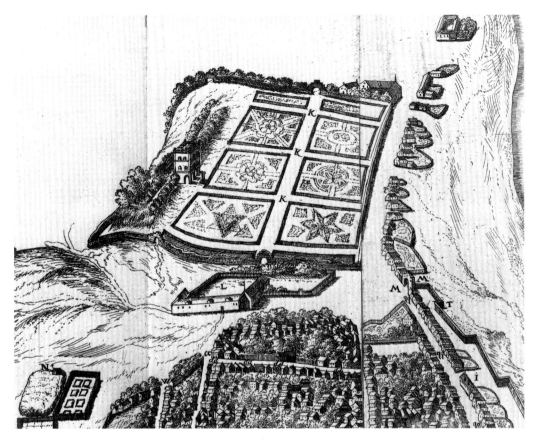

Lundegaard (Lunde-have) and the inn, Lundegaard Kro, according to Peder Hansen Resen's *Atlas Danicus*, 1625–88, unpublished in his lifetime. In a diary kept by a Frenchman named Josias Mercer in 1588, mention is made of Lundehave and the fact that "the King was wont to rest here after his burdensome worries".

Sleeping within my orchard

Yet another small detail comes into the picture in connection with Frederik II's garden at Lundehave. The whole crux of Hamlet's terrible situation is established by the Ghost when he tells his son how and where he was murdered:

> Sleeping within my orchard,
> My custom always of the afternoon,
> Upon my secure hour thy uncle stole
> With juice of cursed hebenon in a vial
> And in the porches of my ears did pour
> The leperous* distilment (I.v.59–64)

There was no orchard or any form of garden at Kronborg Castle, exposed as it was on a promontory and battered by the waves in all seasons. But it was well known that both Frederik II and Christian IV

* **leperous** creating scales on the skin as in leprosy

liked to retire to Lundegaard for an afternoon nap as a respite from for-
malities at court.

It has therefore been suggested that this little detail, like so many
others, could have come to Shakespeare's ears while he was in Elsinore
and that he subsequently incorporated it in the play. This idea became
so strong during the nineteenth century that the garden became known,
especially among English visitors and Shakespearean pilgrims to
Elsinore, as 'Hamlet's Garden'.

I lov'd Ophelia

It has been contended that the very small number of Danish names
– or names that could conceivably have been derived from Danish –
is evidence that "points conclusively to the fact that [Shakespeare]
never set foot on Danish ground" (Cay Dollerup, 1975).

However, first-hand experience of Danish names might have been
the very reason for Shakespeare's wariness of them. In the normal way,
having taken so much trouble to introduce many other details of local
Danish colour, one would think that he would have been only too willing to use Danish names as well.

But it was not so simple. To start with, he obviously had to avoid the
name of the King of Denmark at the time, Christian, and of his father,
Frederik. On the other hand he had to be sure that the names he chose
would be recognizable and understandable to Elizabethan audiences.
But he would have immediately discovered a serious problem: in many
cases it is by no means clear (to non-Scandinavians) whether a Danish
name is male or female.

A visit to Denmark during which he actually heard Danish names
pronounced might have filled him with even more dismay. In the case
of possible names for male characters, how could he expect his audiences to react to Mogens (which rhymes with 'moans'), Bent, Anders,
Didrik, Sivert or Ove, let alone expect actors to learn how to pronounce them? And as for female characters, how would Danish names
like Helvig, Mette or Sidsel have sounded in English ears? Would not
the lines:

> I lov'd Ophelia. Forty thousand brothers
> Could not with all their quantity of love
> Make up my sum.   (V.i.264–266)

have lost something of their magic if he had written "I lov'd Ingeborg" or some other perhaps typical but (but in English ears) rather unmelodious Danish name?

It has also been noted that Shakespeare never once refers to the castle at Elsinore by its Danish name, Kronborg, and that this again is decisive proof that he could never have visited Elsinore personally. But perhaps the same consideration applies: it was a relatively new name (not introduced by Frederik II until 1585) and therefore would have been unfamiliar to London audiences. Besides, how was it to be pronounced? Could he be forgiven for avoiding it deliberately?

A rat! Dead for a ducat, dead

Also in the area sometimes described as 'negative' or 'missing' evidence are Shakespeare's references to money. It has been pointed out that nowhere in *Hamlet* does he make any mention of the names of specifically Danish coins in use at the time: the *daler*, the *mark*, the *skilling* or the *hvid*. This has provoked some rather sweeping conclusions, for example that "we may safely assume that Shakespeare knew nothing of the Danish monetary system … and this is probably one of the best proofs that he was not personally familiar with Denmark" (Cay Dollerup, 1975).

However, the fact that Shakespeare avoided using these names of Danish coins by no means proves that he was ignorant of their existence, for they will have presented the same problem as Danish personal names: Elizabethan audiences could not be expected to recognize them. Thus *daler* was unacceptable (besides, how would actors pronounce it?) and to use one of the various English spellings (dollar, dolour, thaler, tallar) would simply destroy the Danish 'flavour' and therefore be pointless.

The other possibility, the mark, would admittedly have been immediately recognizable as denoting a coin, but by no means necessarily a
Danish one — in fact on the contrary: Shakespeare had often used the
mark as a clearly English monetary unit in earlier plays. In *King John*
(1596), for example, the King makes a handsome offer to increase his
daughter's dowry by

> Full thirty thousand marks of English coin
>
> (II.i.530)

As in virtually all Shakespeare's plays in a foreign setting, most
references to sums of money in *Hamlet* are expressed in ducats, for
example when Hamlet observes that while his father lived there were
those who would give

> twenty, forty, fifty, a hundred ducats apiece for
> his portrait in little
>
> (II.ii.361—62)

and when he thrusts his rapier through the arras and kills Polonius,
crying:

> A rat! Dead for a ducat, dead
>
> (III.iv.23)

Although consistently intent on introducing Danish local colour of
one kind or another, Shakespeare obviously also had other considera-
tions to keep in mind such as metre, euphony or alliteration. These
must often have taken precedence over mere documentary accuracy.
Can one blame him for rejecting "Dead for a mark" or "Dead for a
thaler"?

Besides, although the name ducat was derived from the Italian
ducato, a ducal coin, it was also given to coins of fine gold minted in
many other European countries, including Denmark.* Here again,
Shakespeare's usage was not only reasonable in the context, but also
both accurate and understandable to contemporary audiences.

* Right up to 1827.

His draughts of Rhenish

There are other areas in which Shakespeare introduced deliberate touches of local colour. For example, in establishing that Hamlet, Horatio and perhaps also Rosencrantz and Guildenstern had been studying at Wittenberg in Germany (mentioned four times in I.ii), he combined his knowledge that the university had been frequently attended by Danish scholars and noblemen towards the end of the sixteenth century with the fact that it was also well known throughout Europe on account of its associations with Martin Luther and the Reformation.

Similarly, in connection with the many references to drunkenness and drinking customs at the Danish court, he also specified early in the play precisely what it was Hamlet's uncle drank in such large quantities. When describing the King's drinking bout to Horatio, Hamlet says:

> And as he drains his draughts of Rhenish down
>
> (I.iv.10)

and much later the Gravedigger recalls that Yorick once

> poured a flagon of Rhenish on my head
>
> (V.i.174)

Rhenish was wine from the Rhine valley in Germany, widely regarded as the finest available and therefore favoured in Denmark by the royal court and the Danish aristocracy. Moreover, at Elsinore there were always plentiful supplies, for the King could always exercise his right of pre-emption and buy up cargoes, regardless of the fact that they might be bound for another destination.

Danskers, Switzers and Barbary horses

When Polonius gives his instructions to Reynaldo he says:

> Inquire me first what Danskers are in Paris
>
> (II.i.7)

By this term Shakespeare obviously meant 'Danes' and believed it was the right word. But in point of fact he was mistaken, for though it certainly means 'Danes' in modern Danish, in his time a 'Dansker' actually meant a person from the Baltic port of Danzig (now Gdansk). However, many people in his audiences would have been under the same delusion, so he would still have achieved his purpose.

Similarly, when the King, on hearing the 'noise within' that heralds the arrival of Laertes bent on vengeance, cries out:

> Where is* my Switzers? Let them guard the door.
>
> (IV.v.97)

Shakespeare intended to convey 'Swiss bodyguards' like those in the service of the Pope and the King of France. This too was a small error, for the kings of Denmark never had Swiss guards, only a small guard of halberdiers, probably German mercenaries. However, the uniforms they wore were rather similar, their colours in both cases being red and yellow (which happened to be the dynastic colours of the royal Danish house of Oldenburg) and the cut was also more or less the same. So the technical difference was negligible; Elizabethan audiences would not have protested.

Even in the very last scene of the play, despite all the terrible conflicts and situations still left to be resolved, Shakespeare continued to introduce local colour. Osric tells Hamlet what has passed between the King and Laertes:

> The King, sir, hath wagered with him six Barbary horses, against the which he hath impawned,** as I take it, six French rapiers and poniards ...   (V.ii.144–46)

Arab, or Barbary, horses were highly valued throughout Europe for their beauty and swiftness, but in this instance what could have prompted Shakespeare to regard six of them as a valuable prize for the outcome of a duel? One fanciful theory that has been put forward is that according to some account books for 1610 the Danish King once

* The singular verb is of the period.

** impawned wagered

had a team of six white Barbary horses whose manes and tails were dyed red, their appearance thus symbolizing the colours of the Danish flag. It has therefore been suggested that a team of horses decorated in this way would be among the King's most prized possessions and therefore an impressive stake. But the fact that the Danish King had a team of this kind in 1610 does not necessarily prove that he also had one ten years earlier.

It has also been asserted that as Denmark was renowned for its skill in breeding horses and exporting them all over Europe, Shakespeare was perhaps aware of this and therefore chose what he felt would represent, from a Danish point of view, a valuable Danish wager.

Sceptics claim on the other hand that perhaps Shakespeare intended no suggestion of local colour at all but simply picked on six Barbary horses as the Danish King's stake – no more, no less.

Her virgin crants

At Ophelia's funeral the priest explains that she is to be buried in the churchyard – despite the suspicion that she may have committed suicide. He adds:

> Yet here she is allowed her virgin crants
> Her maiden strewments and the bringing home
> Of bell and burial   (V.i.226–28)

The word 'crants' (which is singular, meaning a garland or ornamental wreath of flowers), derives from the old German and Danish *Kran(t)z*. Apparently it was not sufficiently familiar to Elizabethan audiences, with the result that in the Folio edition of 1623 the phrase was amended to 'her virgin rites'.

The practice of carrying a garland of this kind before the coffin and afterwards hanging it in the church was common not only in northern Europe but also in England. Shakespeare's use of 'crants' was presumably a deliberately inserted Danish word to give a touch of local colour. But was it the sort of word actor colleagues who had visited Elsinore would have been likely to tell him about? Is it perhaps more likely that he had *heard* it used?

When the Queen scatters flowers on Ophelia's grave she laments:

> I thought thy bride-bed to have deck'd, sweet maid
> And not have strew'd thy grave   (V.i.238–39)

It has been suggested that this is yet another carefully introduced Danish detail, for although the custom of having a ceremonially deco- rated bridal bed as part of a marriage ceremony (in addition to the bridal bed proper) was widespread in Protestant Scandinavia and Germany during the greater part of the sixteenth century, it would not have been very familiar to Elizabethan audiences, and that its inclusion could therefore indicate that Shakespeare had either witnessed a cere- mony of this kind – such as the famous occasion at Elsinore in 1585, when Princess Anna was married to James VI of Scotland by proxy – or at least been given first-hand reports of it by someone who had.

However, this suggestion could be disproved by the fact that Shake- speare had already referred to the same custom and used the same turn of phrase much earlier, in *Romeo and Juliet* (1594–95), when Paris, similarly scattering flowers on Juliet's grave, says:

> Sweet flower, with flowers thy bridal bed I strew
>
> (V.iii.12)

The breathing time of day

In the last scene of the play, after receiving Osric's message about the King's wager, Hamlet prefaces his answer by saying:

> Sir, I will walk here in the hall. If it please his Majesty, it is the
> breathing time of day with me.   (V.ii.171)

Shakespeare's use of the phrase 'breathing time' is generally accepted to mean 'time for exercise'. But in the normal way, it might be assumed that anybody wanting to get some exercise, to 'go for a breather', even in the winter, would do so in the fresh air. By letting Hamlet state clearly that he intends to do so 'here in the hall', it has been suggested that Shakespeare was deliberately displaying his knowledge of the fact that the Great Hall at Elsinore Castle was the longest in Europe, that Elsinore was a terribly cold place in the winter, and that anyone bent on going for a walk would not dream of doing so on the ramparts at the mercy of the Danish winter – howling winds, snowstorms, or pouring rain – and instead would welcome the possibility of striding up and down this famous hall. To justify this intention to 'take a breather' indoors Shakespeare again emphasizes how cold Elsinore was in the winter. Earlier in the scene Hamlet has assured Osric

> 'tis very cold, the wind is northerly.   (V.ii.95)

and Osric immediately concedes that

> It is indifferent cold, my lord, indeed.

Could it have been common practice for other members of the Danish court to take their morning 'breathers' in the wintertime striding up and down the Great Hall in preference to out of doors on the frosty, windswept ramparts? If so, was it the sort of thing Shakespeare's actor colleagues would have mentioned to him in London?

Could all these details just have been hearsay, or could some of them perhaps have been based on personal experience? As yet, no conclusive evidence has come to light to prove that Shakespeare either did or did not visit Elsinore, so the door is still ajar. As the Player King observes:

> ... 'tis a question left us yet to prove. (III.ii.197)

PART THREE

A sea of troubles

Nordic rivalry

The seventeenth century had started so splendidly for Elsinore. The number of ships obediently calling in to pay their Sound Dues increased steadily year by year and the town prospered accordingly. Wealthy merchants built fine houses for themselves and invested large sums in bold commercial ventures. The money kept rolling in and everyone was happy. By 1625 Elsinore had a population of close on 10,000 inhabitants and was the second largest town in Denmark.

But this blissful situation was to be repeatedly interrupted either by war or the plague. In the course of just over a hundred years after Shakespeare wrote *Hamlet*, Denmark and Sweden fought no less than six wars against each other in what appeared to be an endless struggle to secure complete control of the Baltic – and every time war broke out it inevitably brought Elsinore's lucrative maritime traffic to a standstill.

In peacetime, the visits to Elsinore of foreign ships and sailors certainly generated affluence, but they also represented a far greater exposure to disease. Denmark suffered repeatedly from epidemics of the plague during this period – about once every ten years – and they were often brought into the country at Elsinore.

The animosity between the Danes and Swedes was deep-rooted. Both nations were convinced that they were unquestionably entitled to naval superiority in the Baltic. Christian IV had inherited from his father, Frederik II, a dream of reconquering Sweden and re-establishing a Nordic union under his own rule. Conversely, his Swedish rival and arch-enemy, Karl IX Gustav, nurtured a hatred for the Danes that was virtually fanatic.

As the years passed, Christian became increasingly convinced that war was an illustrious adventure in which he would be able to make a fine name for himself. He saw little point in repeated attempts at

The two rival Nordic power blocs at the beginning of the seventeenth century.

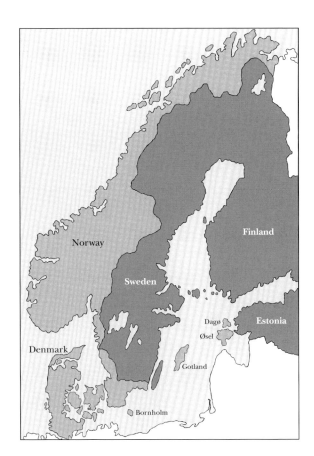

arbitration as long as the Swedish King merely continued to perpetrate 'scoundrelly' acts of piracy against Danish merchantmen and other illegal forms of plundering.

Christian also felt that his regal reputation was at stake, and that he must take some action. He was in a curiously awkward position. Whereas he was free to spend the income he obtained from the Sound Dues at Elsinore as he thought fit, he was not entitled to wage war on another country without the express approval of his Council.

But he had an unusual card up his sleeve. He happened to be not only King of Denmark but also Duke of the provinces of Schleswig and Holstein in northern Germany. While the Council was entitled to control his actions as King, it had no say in what he chose to do as Duke.

Christian decided to play this card adroitly. He informed the Council that he had conferred with God and then decided, with God's full approval, to declare war, both on land and at sea, with the aim of

Christian IV,
King of Denmark
and Norway.
Engraving by
Lucas Kilianus
Augustanus, 1621.

SERENISSIMVS AC POTENTISSIMVS PRINCEPS AC DOMINVS DN. CHRISTIANVS IV. REX DANIÆ ET NORWEGIÆ &c.

Despicio Fatum, fortunam sperno sinistram,
Spe patiens tumidas frango utriusq́ minas.
Fors fera mitescet, mitescet flebile fatum:
Excipient curas gaudia longa meas.
Ejusdem Regiæ Majestati humilime sculpens dicat, consecrat Lucas Kilianus Augustanus.

forcing the Swedish King either to bow to the authority of the Danish Crown or at least mend his evil ways. He informed the Council that if they refused to authorize him to make war on Sweden he intended do so in his alternative capacity as Duke of Schleswig-Holstein – and added, with a swift display of business acumen, that if his venture produced any fruitful results he would keep them strictly to himself and not permit the kingdom of Denmark to benefit from them in any way.

The Council saw there was little more to discuss. As they phrased their formal reply: "We observe that whether we approve or disapprove, Your Majesty is bent on this war." Their last hope was that Almighty God might bring His Majesty to his senses, but they were disappoint-ed. In 1611 Christian levied heavy extra taxes all over the country and also, as "a temporary measure", raised the Sound Dues. He then made a formal declaration of war on Sweden.

The Sound Dues, Elsinore's gold mine, proved at times to be a mixed blessing. Whenever the Danish King was short of money there was an understandable temptation to raise the tariffs. It was so easy – a stroke of the pen – and he repeatedly succumbed to it.* In due course the King came close to strangling the goose that was laying the golden eggs. His meddling was to prove disastrous, not only for Elsinore but for Denmark as a whole.

Single-handed combat

Christian's primary objective in his first war was to conquer the Swedish port of Kalmar on the Baltic coast, including its strong fortress.

Unfortunately the campaign was inadequately organized, with the result that food, gunpowder and ammunition were soon in short sup-ply. The Swedish army's resistance proved much greater than expect-ed. The whole project was moreover extremely expensive – somehow there was never quite enough money. This was particularly serious, for among the major outlays involved in waging war at the time was that

* Many other beneficial little adjustments were so easy to make. For example, in the case of grain, the levy was made per last, a unit of measure normally rated at 24 barrels. But Christian decided at one point to halve it to 12 barrels. It was a quick way of doubling his income.

"The Kingdome of
Denmarke, augmented
by John Speede, 1626"

THE KINGDOME OF DENMARKE augmented by Iohn Speede. & are to be sold in pops head Alley by: G. Humble.

Noble Mans Wife

Marchant.

Husumana Woman

Ditmarschena Woman

Stapelhallema Woman

Coman German miles

Evert Symons z. Hamers veldt sculp.

of hiring mercenaries to do the actual fighting. But mercenaries were professional soldiers who stood no nonsense. If they were not paid promptly they had two simple remedies: they either stopped fighting or went over to the enemy. At one time Christian owed his soldiers a whole month's wages, and the situation became precarious. But at the last moment a Danish fleet arrived in time to relieve the land forces. Kalmar Castle capitulated and Christian was widely acclaimed for his magnificent victory.

However, the circumstances under which this victory was achieved produced yet another problem. It appeared that the capitulation, far from being a straightforward and honourable military defeat, was a rather irregular affair. Christian IV had managed to strike an underhand bargain with the Swedish commander-in-chief of the fortress: in return for his surrender, Christian promised to reward him with the title deed to a handsome estate in Holstein, plus a lump sum in cash.

The old Swedish King, Karl IX Gustav, was incensed. He wrote an angry letter declaring that Christian had "not behaved like an honest and Christian king" but succeeded in conquering the town of Kalmar and its castle solely "by dint of treachery". In Karl's view, there was only one answer to this dispute between the two great Nordic kingdoms. In the manner of the ancient Goths, their respective monarchs must confront each other on the battlefield and engage in single-handed combat, armed only with a rapier and poniard. God Almighty would decide the outcome.

For Christian it was a most awkward situation. By this time he was a relatively athletic man of thirty-four and would probably have had little difficulty in fighting a rapier duel and defeating an old Swedish dodderer aged sixty. But what honour would he gain by it? Besides, while the situation bore a certain resemblance to the last scene in *Hamlet*, in this case the Danish king's wager was not just six Barbary horses but his entire kingdom. Dare he risk it? Supposing God were to move in one of His mysterious ways?

Christian decided that discretion was the better part of valour. He wrote an insulting letter to the Swedish King, mockingly dismissing

The Round Tower of Copen-
hagen, built by Christian IV
(against expert advice) as an
astronomical observatory. The
whole ambitious project was
started in 1637 but was still unfin-
ished at the king's death in 1648.
It was immortalized many years
later in Hans Christian Andersen's
fairy-tale *The Tinder-Box*, where
the dog sitting on the money-chest
full of gold has "eyes as big as
the Round Tower".

the proposal of a duel as the delirious notion of an old fool who obviously needed to have his head examined by a good physician.

The Swedish King died a few months later. The war dragged on
inconclusively and Christian saw that his dream of conquering
the whole of Sweden was beyond his reach. Finally, all concerned
– including Christian himself – were anxious to see hostilities brought
to an end. By the terms of the peace treaty signed in 1613 Sweden agreed
to pay an indemnification of one million rix-dollars.

Elsinore welcomed the prospect of renewed maritime trading.

Money to spend

Within the next few years Christian IV became one of the richest monarchs in Europe. His income from the Sound Dues almost doubled as a result of a tremendous boom in Baltic trading. He could also look forward to the prospect of Sweden's war indemnification being paid in instalments over a six-year period. With so much money at his disposal it is understandable that he found many ways of spending it. In the course of his reign he expanded Copenhagen to twice its former size, founded new towns and fortresses throughout his kingdoms, embarked on various commercial and industrial ventures, sponsored expeditions to Greenland and even attempted to find a passage to China and India round the north of America. He modernized and expanded the Danish navy, built the largest and most modern naval arsenal in Europe, a new Stock Exchange, an observatory (famed as Copenhagen's Round Tower) and also several splendid palaces and buildings, many of which still stand today as part of Denmark's cultural heritage. He was meticulously attentive to detail in all his affairs – more than 3,000 of his letters have been preserved.

One particularly hazardous venture, however, proved to be unwise. He became involved in the Thirty Years' War (1618–48), which at the time was engulfing the whole of central Europe. He suffered humiliating military defeat at the hands of General Tilly in Western Germany in 1626, after which the whole of the Jutlandic peninsula was occupied by German troops. This time Denmark was forced to pay heavy war indemnifications. It was a serious blow, not only to Christian's pride but also to the country's finances.

Engulfed in flames

The castle at Elsinore had long been an awe-inspiring symbol of the Danish King's power, affluence and inalienable command of the Baltic. No ship dared sail past without dipping its flag and striking its topsails. No wonder Christian IV regarded it as "the finest jewel in his crown".

But in 1629 the whole building went up in flames. Apparently the repeated cannon-healths and volleys of shot fired from the big square gun tower had weakened its structure. Repairs were urgently needed. Reinforcement of the walls often involved the fastening of iron tie-bars, a process which required lead to be melted in a crucible over a little fire, which at the end of the day would be dowsed with a bucket or two of water.

But one September evening, despite this precaution, the embers continued to smoulder. A strong south-westerly wind suddenly caused them to blaze up. The timberwork caught fire, rafters and spires collapsed, the beautiful sheet-copper roofing melted and the castle's cannon and bells were ruined by the intense heat. All the interiors were ravaged by the flames excepting those on the ground floor and the chapel, which was saved by its vaulted ceilings. Quantities of furnish-ings and accessories were burnt, including over 200 tables and dozens of paintings – though there is no record of any of the famous tapestries having been lost, perhaps because they were relatively easy to rescue; many of them had moreover already been moved to other palaces and houses.

The outer walls remained standing, and luckily the flames never reached the huge gunpowder store, for had they done so the whole castle would have been blown up and little might have been left even of Elsinore itself.

Christian was anxious to restore the fortress at once, for to leave it as an abandoned ruin was unthinkable. The Council protested that the nation was impoverished after the King's ill-fated participation in the Thirty Years' War in Germany. But Christian pointed out, like his father before him, that all expenses could be covered by income from the Sound Dues, which he would quite simply, once again, double "as a temporary measure". This time he was at least courteous enough to ask the Dutch commissary in Denmark for his approval (for the Dutch would suffer most from the increases), pointing out that the fortress was, after all, of great importance to his constant task of restraining the activities of pirates. The Dutch generously agreed.

It took Christian more than ten years to rebuild and repair his father's beloved castle at Elsinore, though he never managed to restore all the interiors to their former splendour.

Despite setbacks and financial difficulties during these years, Chris-tian was determined to keep up appearances. In 1634 he celebrated the wedding of his son Christian and Princess Magdalena Sibylla of Saxony with a display of unprecedented sumptuousness. It was not just to please his son; his principal aim was to demonstrate to the rest of Europe that he was still, despite his lack of success in the European wars, an incontestably powerful and affluent monarch.

A rude awakening

Christian IV's next step with the aim of bolstering his finances was to introduce yet another series of toll increases at Elsinore. Even though these were made at a time when trade in the Baltic was decreasing, this drastic step enabled him to treble his income from about 200,000 rix-dollars in 1636 to over 600,000 rix-dollars in 1639.

The Danish King's repeated interference with the Sound Dues had often caused irritation, especially among the English and the Dutch, who were normally the ones to suffer most. But this time the severity of the additional charges and other related burdens produced such serious political animosity that the Netherlands decided to enter into a distinctly anti-Danish alliance with Sweden. By 1643 the Swedes decided that if Christian IV's behaviour was ever going to be curbed it could only be by outright military defeat. This time they were the ones to declare war.

The successful battles fought by Sweden in Poland and Germany during the Thirty Years' War had given them control of large parts of the Baltic coast. Sweden's aim now was not only to put a definitive end to Denmark's naval control of the Baltic but also to conquer at least the Danish provinces in the south of the Scandinavian peninsula – Halland, Blekinge and Skåne – so as to move the Swedish border right down to the Sound. Ultimately, Sweden would prefer to wipe Denmark off the map as an independent nation and instead reinstate a Nordic Union under Swedish control.

Denmark was attacked on two fronts: a Swedish army marched southwards into Skåne, while Swedish troops in Germany marched northwards into Schleswig-Holstein and occupied the whole of Jutland.

A naval battle was fought between Danish and Swedish fleets in the summer of 1644 but produced no clear result except that Christian IV, on board his flagship "Trefoldigheden" (Holy Trinity), was badly wounded and lost an eye. After being bandaged he insisted coura-geously on continuing as Commander-in-Chief of the fleet, thereby earning immortal glory in the eyes of his countrymen.

But then something far more serious happened. In August 1644 a fleet of Dutch merchantmen convoyed by warships reached Elsinore and then simply continued southwards past the castle without making any attempt to dip their flags or strike their topsails. Kronborg's guns roared, but in vain: the fleet sailed on, untouched and undeterred.

It came as a shock. For more than 200 years the guns of Elsinore (said to number more than a hundred) had represented an internationally respected deterrent, to be ignored only at one's peril.

Of course it was common knowledge that the range of cannon of the period was no more than a few hundred metres with any degree of accuracy. It was also realized that by raising the angle of elevation of a gun barrel a cannon-ball could be sent flying further, but that the higher the angle, the greater the tendency of the cannon-ball to 'drop into' – rather than strike – the hull of a ship, so that the damage caused was not always so serious. But ballistics was still far from being an exact science, so the worst was to be expected. The very unpredictability of the striking power of the guns of the period had long contributed to instil both fear and obedience.*

On this occasion, however, the Dutch fleet had dared to call the Danes' bluff, thereby proving that the castle's bark was worse than its bite. They simply sailed past, unhindered, and joined up with a Swedish fleet, after which a final naval battle took place in which the Danes were severely defeated. Although the Swedes were not in a position, even after this victory, to enforce the complete subjugation of Denmark, the Danes were forced by the terms of a peace treaty signed at Brömsebro in 1645 to surrender two large provinces in Norway and two islands of vital naval importance in the Baltic, Gotland and Ösel (the latter is now part of present-day Estonia). Another Danish province was to be made over to Sweden for a period of thirty years as a security.

Never before in its history had Denmark had to pay such a high price for peace. The gradual dismemberment of the once powerful twin kingdoms of Denmark and Norway had commenced. From having been one of Europe's richest monarchs, Christian IV gradually found himself in financial difficulties. At one point he was reduced to pawning the crown that had been specially made for his coronation in 1596.

He died in 1648 aged 70.

* A story was told about one of Elsinore's biggest and most powerful guns, nick-named Skægget (Beardie). It was said that a highly skilled gunner once took aim with it at a cow in a field on the other side of the straits (almost five kilometres away!) and managed to knock it over without hurting the milkmaid or even spilling the milk.

A fateful turning-point

Ten years later, in 1658, the defensive strength of Elsinore's famous castle was put to a real test for the first time, with disastrous results: it was besieged, captured and occupied by Swedish troops. The circum-stances leading up to this turning-point in Elsinore's and Denmark's history were the result of a military manoeuvre of astonishing boldness.

Christian IV's son Frederik III inherited two war-weary kingdoms that were menaced by Sweden's steadily increasing power and by the generally unstable political climate in Europe. He set about restoring order and was reasonably successful, but with the accession to the throne of Sweden in 1654 of an experienced army commander, Karl X Gustav, he was faced with a situation that soon became precarious.

At this time Sweden had an army in the north of Germany. Main-taining an army was expensive. The Swedish monarch's problem was whether to disband it or use it for some practical purpose, such as attacking another country. The latter course seemed preferable, because the cost of feeding and billeting it would then be met – as in the normal course of successful aggressive warfare – by the country in question. He had two possibilities: Poland or Denmark.

Sweden felt closed in and obstructed by the naval power of the twin kingdoms of Denmark and Norway. To demonstrate his country's superiority, Sweden's warrior monarch decided to attack Poland, and was so successful that within a few months he had occupied both Warsaw and Cracow. It then became clear to everybody that Denmark would be next on his list.

The Danish King therefore decided in turn that attack would be the best means of defence. He was supported by his Council and at the time there seemed to be many sound reasons for taking the decision – there was hardly any alternative – but it proved to be one of the most fateful in Denmark's history.

Denmark's ice-bound islands

Frederik III declared war on Sweden on 1 June 1657, and the Swedish King, Karl X Gustav, reacted promptly. He sent an expeditionary force to attack Denmark from the south and within less than six months had occupied the entire Jutlandic peninsula. But there he was brought to a halt by water, for in addition to this peninsula Denmark consists of about 500 islands of varying sizes.

In the normal way these Danish islands could be attacked only by transporting troops by sea. This presupposed naval superiority, which Karl Gustav did not have. But as the winter began to close in with unusual harshness it gave him a daring idea. If the waters separating all these Danish islands were to freeze to solid ice, perhaps he would be able to march his army across from one island to another all the way to Copenhagen?

In the course of January 1658, Karl Gustav gathered a force of about 6,000 cavalry and 2,500 infantry and began to test the ice in various places. He soon discovered that the shortest distance across a stretch of ice was not necessarily the safest, for the narrower the channel the stronger the current – and the greater the likelihood of pack ice and treacherous thin ice.

The Little Belt at its narrowest point between Jutland and the island of Funen is only about one kilometre wide, but Karl Gustav found he would have to risk a much longer route further south: first a distance of three kilometres to a very small island and then another nine kilometres across to a much larger one, Funen.

Horses with spiked shoes to prevent them from slipping on the ice. Woodcut in Olaus Magnus, *Historia de gentibus septentrionalibus* (1555), Book 1, Chapter 25.

1:1

L   a   a   l   a   n   d

Sænideos quid Roma tuos, quid Græca vetustas
Laurigeros iactas, nomina magna, duces?
Maior in Arctoo consurgit gloria mundo,
Subque Lycaonio Sidere vincit honos.
Rex Suéonum CAROLUS GUSTAVUS vindice ferro
Hostes prosternens æquora transit eques.
Admittúnt placide Regem Neptunia regna.

Karl X Gustav's army
crossing the frozen
waters of the Great
Belt, 7th February 1658.

Victoremque stupet Cimbrica vincta Thetis.
Successus tantos veniens mirabitur ætas,
Nec facile inveniet transitis iste fidem.
Calcarunt fluvios alii Mare sternitur illi;
Talis Hyperboreo laurea digna Duce.
Esse DEO carum quis post hæc ambiget illum
Naturæ illustrat quem famulantis opus!
J. Bergenhielm.

He was understandably cautious, continually sending out small patrols to test the thickness of the ice. Some came back and some did not. On one occasion two whole companies (about 100 cavalrymen) and a couple of sledges, including his own royal sledge (he was not on it) simply disappeared in the icy waters. But he went on probing in the hope of finding places where the ice would hold.

Many other precautions were taken. Cavalrymen were not to ride their horses but lead them by the bridle, and they were to spread out and keep their distance – also to render them less vulnerable to fire from Danish guns.

Gradually, he found what seemed to be safe routes. But, even when a large expanse of ice was apparently thick and dependable, its resiliency would often cause it to sag in the middle under the weight of hundreds and hundreds of horses and men – and their weapons. Understandably, fear was widespread, not least among the horses.

News of what the Swedish King was attempting to do gradually spread. The Danes were shocked. It was all very well to march on the ice of a frozen lake, but to risk crossing a frozen belt of water with a strong current flowing underneath was regarded as sheer madness.

But Karl Gustav persevered and reached the island of Funen, which is in the middle of Denmark and about 100 kilometres wide. He marched across it, fighting some small battles on the way, but the Danish defenders were totally unprepared for this invasion and more-over greatly outnumbered. When the last of these skirmishes had been won and the few remaining Danish troops taken prisoner, Karl Gustav, having lost his own sledge, leapt onto a farmer's shouting "This shall be my war chariot!"

Then – his ultimate audacity, completely against the advice of his generals – Karl Gustav insisted on leading his army even across the Great Belt. He chose a southerly route, first over to the island of Langeland and then – the longest, most incredible stretch of all, 15 kilometres – to Lolland.

How could these Swedish troops retain their faith in their King's judgement? How did they manage to keep their spirits up? Even when they were marching on terra firma it was bitterly cold and the snow lay deep. Conditions were miserably arduous in every way. Supplies of food and other necessities were highly irregular as most of the army baggage had been left behind in Jutland.

Karl X Gustav, King of Sweden. Engraving by Petrus van Schuppen, 1663, after a painting by David Klööker.

The French ambassador (who had been obliged to accompany the Swedish monarch throughout this mad march) noted in his diary that beer and wine casks had to be hacked open with mattocks and their frozen contents broken into lumps and thawed over a fire, after which "the taste left much to be desired".

Crossing the ice at night brought its own terrors, for there was the constant fear of losing one's bearings, straying onto a thin patch and never being seen again. But Karl Gustav continued resolutely from island to island, until finally, on 11 February, he reached Zealand and could take up a position within a suitable distance of his objective: Copenhagen, the Danish capital.

The Danish Council was in a state of panic. Nothing like this had ever happened before. Nobody could remember such a terrible winter or such a hard frost. So, just as had been the case thirteen years earlier, they were obliged to negotiate peace terms as fast as possible.

A treaty was signed at the end of February 1658. Sweden's demands were harsh. The Danes were to cede their three provinces in the south of the Scandinavian peninsula (Skåne, Halland and Blekinge), the island of Bornholm in the Baltic and two Norwegian provinces. All in all, Denmark lost about a third of its entire territory.

The siege of Elsinore Castle

So far the treaty was a triumph for the Swedish King. But certain clauses in it gave rise to haggling over their interpretation, and he was still faced with the old problem of maintaining his army. The peace treaty stipu- lated, amongst other things, that Sweden's troops were to be withdrawn from Denmark. But what was he to do with them? Besides, there was another gnawing thought: Denmark was still an independent nation. Had he made a big mistake in signing the treaty? Would it not have been better to conquer the whole country once and for all and then sim- ply incorporate Jutland and all those 500 little islands as a province of Sweden?

Once the plan had taken root in his mind he lost no time. In the summer of 1658, only a few months after signing the peace treaty, Karl

Engraving by Erik Dahlbergh illustrating the salutes fired when the victorious Swedish King left Elsinore after capturing the Castle in 1658.

X Gustav broke its terms, landed a new army of 6,000 men at Korsør on the west coast of Zealand and marched towards Copenhagen. This was to be the *coup de grâce*.

The Swedish King made no formal declaration of war. By diplomatic standards of the day his invasion was therefore an act of flagrant aggression. This in itself was likely to provoke strong international reaction, so he knew he would have to act fast. In order to secure his ends he would have to besiege and capture not only Copenhagen but also the formidable castle at Elsinore, which represented the key to the Sound and the Baltic. He assumed that Copenhagen would be an easy prize, but that Kronborg Castle, whose strength was legendary, might be more difficult. Both assumptions proved to be wrong.

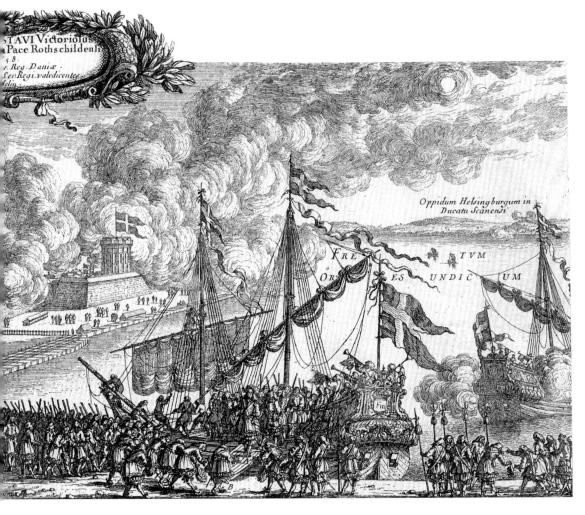

Karl Gustav sent a general with an expeditionary force of about 3,000 soldiers to Elsinore, where they pitched camp outside the walls of the castle in readiness to attack. Here the Swedish general was approached, to his surprise, by a delegation sent by the burgomaster and town councillors of Elsinore. They politely requested Swedish 'protection' and assured the general that he could easily capture the castle, for it was manned only by about 250 soldiers and a few artillerymen.

This obviously stamped the people of Elsinore as traitors to their country's cause, but perhaps they had little option. The town itself had no defenceworks whatsoever, and a large proportion of its citizens were moreover English, Dutch or German who cared little one way or the other whether the town ended up in Danish or Swedish hands.

So the Swedish general launched a series of systematic bombard-
ments and attacks, and after three weeks the castle's commandant
capitulated.

The Swedish King moved in triumphantly the very next day. He
immediately gave orders to commence repairs to the castle, which had
suffered considerable damage, for he wanted it to be a new royal and
impressive residence for his Queen, Leonora, as soon as he had finished
conquering the rest of Denmark.

The storming of Copenhagen

Kronborg's reputation was soon to suffer another blow. Although
during the previous war between Denmark and Sweden the Dutch
had sided with the Swedes in protest against Christian IV's raising
of Sound Dues, they now regarded the prospect of Sweden being in
complete command of the Sound instead with equal dismay. As
Copenhagen was now threatened by Karl Gustav's impending siege
they immediately sent a fleet to bring urgently needed reinforcements
and supplies to the beleaguered Danish capital.

Karl X Gustav was prepared for this development, but awaited
it with tranquillity. After all, for the first time in history, after years of
conflict, Sweden was now at last in supreme command of fortresses on
both sides of the famous straits at Elsinore.

Just as a hostile Dutch fleet had done fifteen years earlier, this time a
friendly Dutch fleet approached Elsinore and, equally unimpeded,
sailed calmly on without dipping their flags or striking their topsails.
The Swedish King personally took aim and fired the first shot at them.
But to no avail. The range and accuracy of the guns proved to be as
unreliable as ever. The Dutch merely steered a course more or less
halfway between the two coasts and passed through untouched. They
were then attacked by a Swedish fleet, but after a six-hour battle
managed to bring the desperately needed reinforcements and supplies
to Copenhagen. Once again it had been conclusively demonstrated
that Elsinore Castle's much-vaunted strength was not really a matter of
serious concern.

Meanwhile Copenhagen, which Karl Gustav fondly imaged would
be simple to conquer, had been consolidating its defences. The Danish

Naval battle between the Swedish and Dutch fleets, 1658. Engraving in Samuel von Pufendorf's history of the wars of Karl X Gustav, published in Latin in 1696.

King was urged to flee but refused. He insisted on having his royal tent pitched on the city's ramparts and is said to have declared dramatically (with a quote from the Book of Job, 29:18) "I shall die in my nest!"

The citizens of Copenhagen, inspired by their monarch's example, suddenly became aware that not only their own lives but Denmark's very existence as a nation was at stake and therefore staunchly determined to die with their King rather than submit to the Swedish aggressor.

Karl Gustav finally stormed Copenhagen on the night of 11 February. Wave after offensive wave was launched, but all were repelled. The following morning the Swedes were obliged to acknowledge their failure and withdraw after having suffered considerable losses.

Denmark's independence was preserved and Sweden's ambitions were thwarted. A peace treaty confirming most of the territorial losses Denmark had already agreed to was concluded in 1660, but Karl X Gustav's signature was not on it; he had died of a heart attack a few months earlier.

The burgomaster of Elsinore and his councillors drew up a list of the expenses incurred by the town in connection with the war. They had had to feed and provide living quarters not only for the commanding officer of the Swedish forces and all his staff, including "many high-ranking officers who did not even have any troops under their command but still insisted on being waited on hand and foot like lords", but also for one cavalry regiment and four infantry regiments, all of which had cost "a most dreadful sum of money". Many fine houses and beautiful buildings had been destroyed in the course of the three-week siege and bombardment. In addition, the ferrymen of Elsinore had also been given the enormous burden of transporting the entire Swedish army back across the Sound to what was now – as had to be bitterly acknowledged – Swedish territory.

All in all the burgomaster worked out that the town's expenses amounted to more than 300,000 rix-dollars, to which had to be added the loss of personal property of all kinds such as "swords, guns, pistols, household goods, bedclothes, copper and pewter utensils", even building materials and boats – to all of which the Swedish troops had apparently helped themselves freely.

War booty had also been seized on a much higher and more sophisticated level. In the course of the conquest and occupation of the rest of Denmark – except for Copenhagen – Karl Gustav, in the customary fashion of victoriously advancing armies, had conducted a systematic programme of looting valuables from Denmark's palaces and manor houses. In many cases the selection was made by his queen, Leonora. Cartloads of works of art, paintings, furniture, even whole precious libraries, were shipped across the Sound and taken to Stockholm.

Leonora also had many valuable works of art removed from Elsinore Castle, including the tapestry banqueting table canopy that Frederik II had commissioned from Hans Knieper and the ornate fountain in the courtyard that had taken Gregorius van der Schardt eight years to make. The canopy is still in Stockholm, but all the fountain's beautiful statues were melted down to make church bells.

Denmark and Sweden had done most of the fighting, but the real victors were Europe's other maritime powers, whose main interest had been to ensure that neither Denmark or Sweden managed to retain command of the straits at Elsinore and thus of all trade in the Baltic. The Sound, which for centuries had been indisputably "the Danish King's waters", had become instead a channel between two rival countries. In the eyes of the Western powers, the endless squabble between the Danes and the Swedes as to who held the command of the Baltic was at an end: the Baltic was part of the European maritime network with equal rights for all. Curiously, however, Denmark's age-old right to demand payment of Sound Dues was not contested.

In one respect the importance of Elsinore Castle was radically changed. Instead of being surrounded by Danish territory on both sides of the straits, its task was now to defend what had become Denmark's easternmost border. This entailed the maintenance of a considerable garrison force of up to about 1,000 soldiers, for whom living quarters had to be found in the homes of the townspeople, who suffered under this additional burden.

The angel of death

Denmark made two attempts to recover the provinces in the south of the Scandinavian peninsula that had been lost as a result of the Swedish King's extraordinary march across the ice. Both involved long, futile wars that lasted four and eleven years respectively (1675–79 and 1709–20). In both cases, Elsinore suffered from all its usual wartime burdens and sacrifices.

Another blow came with an epidemic of the plague that had started in Constantinople in 1704 and slowly moved northwards. It reached Elsinore in 1710 (possibly brought by ships from Baltic ports) and spread remorselessly.

Plague-stricken houses were marked with a big white cross. All household chattels were to be washed with lye and salt water. Attempts to disinfect bedclothes were made by fumigating them with the smoke of juniper twigs, sulphur, resin — even gunpowder. Coins were often kept in a bucket of water full of onions, presumably in the hope of disinfecting them.

There was no known cure, though many possibilities were tried, such as bleeding and emetics. But nothing helped. Superstition was rife. A practice rumoured to be effective was throwing a live cat into the grave of the deceased. In one case at Elsinore a woman carefully laid her dead sister on her side in her coffin in the pious hope that this would help to ward off the plague. But it came to the ears of the local vicar, who protested vehemently and gave instructions for the deceased to be disinterred, straightened out and reburied "on her back, like any decent Christian".

Within a year the plague had wiped out more than a third of the town's population. An entry in the parish register grimly recorded that they had been "torn away by the heavy hand of the Angel of Death as God's punishment for our misdeeds".

It was one of the greatest misfortunes Elsinore had ever suffered. The town was completely paralysed, and for many years afterwards more than half its houses and cottages were to remain derelict and uninhabited. Its position as the second largest town in Denmark was lost forever; its population was reduced to little more than 2,000.

Peace and prosperity

For the first time in hundreds of years, Denmark then found itself enjoying a long period of peace. European trading activities expanded steadily throughout the world and Elsinore gradually recovered.

Around 1750, the annual number of ships calling in to pay their Sound Dues was between 4,000 and 5,000. Within the next fifty years this figure had almost trebled. Ships' captains of all nationalities became increasingly dependent on their consuls and the customs clearance assistance they were able to arrange. The whole system of declaring cargoes and calculating the various tariffs had become so complicated that only specialized agents were able to handle the paperwork.

Only a nominal fee would be charged for handling a ship's customs clearance paperwork – which might well take a day or two – but there was a tacitly understood bargain: in return, the consul or agent expected the captain to buy everything he needed in the way of provisions from the agency's own shipchandler: pickled meat and fish, dried peas and beans, butter, sugar, salt, beer, wine, brandy – and also many practical items such as rope, sailcloth, tar, timber and other necessities.

It was all a mutually profitable arrangement. A ship's captain would therefore be most warmly welcomed in the home of his consul or shipping agent. He would be offered a comfortable bedroom and invited to dine at the family table for as long as he was in port (which depended partly on how many other ships were competing for attention but also on the wind) and his host would often show how much he appreciated having the captain as his guest (and customer) by presenting him with an expensive gift, such as a punchbowl from the Royal Copenhagen Porcelain Manufactory, decorated with a splendid picture of his ship – perhaps with Elsinore Castle in the background – and its name in gold lettering. These gifts became well known in England as 'Elsinore bowls'.

By this time England's merchant navy was much larger than Holland's. During the sixteenth and seventeenth centuries Elsinore had often been referred to by the Dutch as 'Little Amsterdam', but in the eighteenth century the town was more often nicknamed 'Little England' on account of the many English ships calling at Elsinore and the increasing numbers of English merchants who had settled in the town to make their fortunes.

There were also Scottish, Dutch and German colonies, but the English, in the customary fashion of Britain's empire-builders all over the world, set particular store by upholding their own customs and life-style in regard to clothing, servants, carriages, horses, social inter-course and, in particular, what they ate and drank. To the puzzlement of their Danish acquaintances, English gentlemen in Elsinore would expect the ladies to withdraw after dinner. They would then call for a decanter of port – which would be replenished more than once in the course of the evening – and continue drinking until lugged off to bed by their servants.

An Elsinore punchbowl.

Gravestone in Elsinore
Cemetery

In many cases the family business was carried on successfully from generation to generation. They built splendid houses and warehouses in the heart of Elsinore close to the waterfront, many of which still stand. Some of these prosperous English merchants also acquired country estates to which they would retire in the summertime, and of course they gave them suitable English names, such as 'Fairyhill' or 'Claythorpe'.

These English families did little to endear themselves to the towns-folk of Elsinore, who often regarded them as unspeakably arrogant. Their behaviour sometimes inspired their Danish servants and clerical staff to ape the lordly ways and sartorial idiosyncrasies of their masters, only to find themselves not only ridiculed by their compatriots but also sneered at by their employers, who would look down their noses and murmur "Ah, there goes Lord Rasmussen …" or "Begad, look at little Lord Larsen!"

In their usual fashion, the English made few efforts to learn Danish. But in the course of time they became so numerous and so powerful that they felt entitled to request permission to build their own church and appoint their own vicar, because – as they complained – they could not understand the sermons preached in Danish churches; their requests were granted.

When members of these families died they were buried in Elsinore Cemetery, but naturally their gravestones would be specially ordered from England. Many of them can still be seen, and some of the names on them recall characters in Jane Austen's novels.

Untenable neutrality

This prosperity continued right through to the end of the eighteenth century, whereupon Elsinore's blissful situation was shattered once again, this time by the Napoleonic Wars. Denmark had long steered a successful policy of neutrality through the complicated intrigues of European power politics, but finally found itself supporting Napoleon, with the result that the British found it necessary to adopt serious counter-measures.

In 1801 a British fleet under Admiral Parker, whose second-in-command was the already renowned Admiral Nelson, hove in sight at Elsinore. It cast anchor and politely sent a signal to the commandant of the castle requesting permission to pass through. But the commandant replied that he could not possibly allow a fleet of warships bound for an unknown destination to pass his guns.

Parker therefore waited for the wind to freshen and then sailed past anyway, hugging the Swedish coast as closely as possible. The guns of Elsinore roared, but once again, just as in similar critical situations in the past, they failed to score any hits. The English fleet returned the fire equally ineffectively, though ironically enough one stray shot did drop out of the blue into the house of the British Consul-General, Nicolas Fenwick.*

* The house still exists and the cannon-ball has been bricked into the wall of the courtyard as a memento.

The fleet sailed on southwards, reached Copenhagen and fought the naval battle best remembered in English history books as the occasion when Nelson put his telescope to his blind eye.

It was an unusual situation. The Danish fleet was still in winter quarters. Most of the crews had been demobilized and the ships dismantled. Volunteers were recruited in haste and guns were mounted in a number of ships which were then warped out of the harbour and anchored in line to form a blockade.

The battle was violent and lasted about five hours. Despite the inferior strength of the Danes and their inability to manoeuvre, Nelson found himself in difficulties on several occasions, which finally prompted Admiral Parker (who is said to have overestimated the danger) to send a signal ordering him to retire. But Nelson, understandably reluctant to forgo the victory he was convinced was within reach, put his telescope to his blind eye and declared, with a display of heroism and what has been termed the playfulness of his nature, "I see no signal." The battle continued, and finally he sent a letter ashore informing the Danish government that if they refused to give up he would set fire to the anchored ships he had captured so far and that he would unfortunately not be able to save their "brave crews". In the face of this harsh threat the Danish Crown Prince felt he had no option but to surrender.

Nelson subsequently declared that the aim of his letter was to show mercy, but in point of fact it seems to have been an artful ruse, because it appeared that at the time the message was sent ashore he had not actually seized any Danish ships at all.

Six years later, scared by the possibility that the still powerful Danish navy might fall into the hands of the Russians and the French (who would have used it to cut off Britain's vital Baltic trade) the English returned with another fleet, landed an army on the east coast of Zealand, encircled Copenhagen, subjected the city to a merciless bombardment and finally secured Denmark's unconditional surrender.

The Danish fleet was commandeered as war booty. Virtually every single warship was sailed northwards through the Sound, past the now silent guns of Elsinore and across the North Sea to England, thus bringing Denmark's once supreme naval command of the Baltic to an ignominious end.

This battery of guns, cast in the late 1760s, is still on the ramparts of Elsinore Castle.

Meanwhile, Elsinore's fortunes had continued to swing in accordance with commercial fluctuations. The Battle of Copenhagen was followed by a peaceful interlude – in 1802 a record total of 12,124 ships called in to pay their Sound Dues. But in 1808, the year after the bombardment of Copenhagen, this figure plummeted to the lowest ever in Elsinore's history: 121.

For a while things simply went from bad to worse. The Danish government had to declare what was popularly known as 'state bankruptcy' in 1813, and a year later Denmark was compelled by the terms of the Treaty of Kiel to hand over Norway to the King of Sweden – just like moving a pawn in a game of chess.

Elsinore's consuls, shipchandlers and customs clearing agents, all of whom had enjoyed such splendid prosperity throughout most of the eighteenth century, were forced out of business. Even the ferrymen, who accounted for about a quarter of the town's indigenous citizenry, were so short of work right up to about 1815 that the authorities agreed that it would be reasonable to grant them dispensation from the obligation to send their children to school, quite simply because they were unable to scrape a livelihood together without their children's help.

Despite all these setbacks, Elsinore recovered. By 1817 the number of ships cleared through customs at Elsinore had already risen to more than 13,000 – though by no means distributed evenly throughout the year. Very few ships called in during the winter, when the straits and the Baltic Sea might be ice-bound for months on end. Even during the summer there could be days when it was impossible to sail through, either because the wind was unfavourable, or because there was no wind at all.*

Traffic was at its most intense between July and September. Sometimes all the ferrymen, clearing agents, shipchandlers, translators, clerks, accountants, book-keepers, apprentices and many others connected with the whole process found themselves having to handle up to two or even three hundred ships a day. The record number was 353 ships on 18 September 1853. That year also marked the largest number of ships in the whole history of the extraordinary arrangement ever to cast anchor at Elsinore in order for their captains to have themselves ferried ashore to pay their Sound Dues: 24,648.

* The nightwatchmen of Elsinore would sing a little verse as they walked through the streets, for example reminding the townsfolk to snuff their candles and dowse their fires. They would then call out the time, and finally say which way the wind (if any) was blowing.

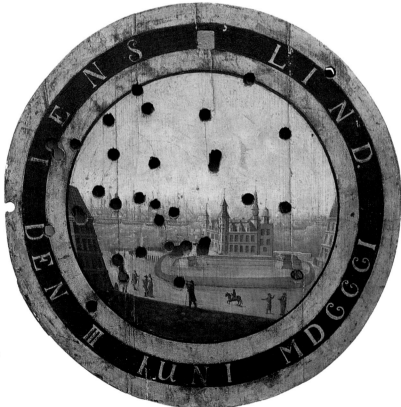

The English fleet passing Elsinore Castle on 30 March 1801. Contemporary painted shooting target, artist unknown.

The end of the game

Four years later it was all over. A major contributory factor was the rapidly increasing development of the steamship to replace the sailing ship. Steamships had no need to wait for a favourable wind. Having to cast anchor at Elsinore and go ashore to pay Sound Dues was therefore increasingly regarded as an intolerable delay.

It was the Americans who upset the apple-cart, declaring that the foundations for extorting the Sound Dues had been laid in "a remote and barbaric age, even before the discovery of America", and that whatever reasons might exist in support of continuing them could have no application to themselves, for "they apply exclusively to the nations of Europe". The USA simply gave Denmark a year's notice, on the expiry of which it saw no reason why it should continue to pay Sound Dues.

There was no conspiracy between the USA and the countries of Europe. On the contrary, the USA's interference in what was regarded as a strictly European problem was resented. An international agreement to abolish Denmark's gold mine was nevertheless signed in 1857.

It was agreed, however, that Denmark should be paid an indemnification for agreeing to give up this age-old source of income. The amount arrived at was 35,000,000 rix-dollars, to be paid by all the maritime nations involved and calculated in proportion to their trade with the Baltic in the course of the past decade or so. Great Britain and Russia bore the brunt: 29 and 28 per cent respectively.

Elsinore felt it should be entitled to at least some share of this indemnification, but the Danish government disagreed, so in the end the town received nothing.

So, after an incredibly lucrative period of more than 400 years, the Sound Dues were finally abolished and the gold mine was closed down.

But that was almost 150 years ago. Elsinore has long since recovered and is well into its fourth period of prosperity. The narrow straits are still the key ferry service point between the Scandinavian peninsula and the rest of Europe. Ferries sail every 20 minutes in both directions and carry about 13 million passengers and almost 2 million motor vehicles a year. Elsinore still has its beautiful Renaissance castle, one of the oldest and best preserved monasteries in northern Europe and a neat little grid of narrow streets (most of them now pedestrian precincts) in the heart of the old part of the town that is still virtually the same as when it was first planned almost six hundred years ago.

But above all, despite the many slings and arrows of outrageous fortune that Elsinore has suffered over the centuries, the one thing that has never dimmed is its fame. The town itself and 'Hamlet's Castle' now draw over 200,000 tourists a year. For however famous Elsinore may have been in Shakespeare's time on account of the Sound Dues and the splendour of the Danish court, there is no mistaking the reason for its fame today.

Illustrations

Bibliography

Andersen, Vilhelm: "Hamlet paa Kronborg", *Et Tiaar*, Gyldendal 1945, pp. 46–51.

Askgaard, Finn and Gunnar Olsen, *En Kamp for Livet. Svenskekrigene 1657–60*, Copenhagen 1958.

Bergsøe, Paul: "Hamlet, Shakespeare og Kronborg", *Udvalgte Skrifter*, Copenhagen 1949.

Braunius & Hohenbergius, *Civitates Orbis Terrarum*, Cologne 1572–1617, I–VI (later edition printed in Amsterdam, n.d., under title *Theatrum praecipuarum urbium positarum ad Septentrionalem Europae Plagam*, usually abbreviated *Theatrum urbium*).

Braun and Hogenberg, *Civitates Orbis Terrarum*, ed. R.A.. Skelton (facsimile edition), Amsterdam 1965.

Brown, Keith : "Shakespeare's Place on the Map", *Shakespeare Studies* IV, 1968 , pp. 160–82.

Christensen, Aksel (*et al.*, eds.): *Danmarks historie*, I–X, Copenhagen 1977–92.

Christensen, Charles: *Kronborg. Frederik II's Renæssanceslot og dets senere Skæbne.* Copenhagen 1950.

Clausen, Julius: "Shakespeare and Elsinore", *American Scandinavian Review*, XII, 1924, pp. 538–43.

Dollerup, Cay: *Denmark, Hamlet and Shakespeare. A Study of Englishmen's Knowledge of Denmark towards the End of the Sixteenth Century with Special Reference to Hamlet*, I–II, Salzburg 1975.

– *Kronborg and Hamlet*, Elsinore, Copenhagen 1989.

Egevang, Robert: *Det gamle Helsingør*, Copenhagen 1977.

Frantzen, Ole L.: *Dansk Landartilleri 1400–2000*, Copenhagen, 1997

Glete, Jan: *Navies and Nations. Warships, Navies and State Building in Europe and America 1500–1860*, I–II, Stockholm 1993.

Gollanz, Sir Israel: *The Sources of 'Hamlet'*, London 1926.

Hibbard, G.R. (ed.): *Hamlet* (The Oxford Shakespeare), Oxford 1987 (1994).

Hill, Charles E.: *The Danish Sound Dues and the Command of the Baltic*, Durham, Carolina 1926.

Holmes, Martin: *The Guns of Elsinore*, London 1964.

Hvass, Lone: *Erik af Pommerns Helsingør*, Elsinore 1996.

– *Klostrets og kirkernes Helsingør*, Elsinore 1997.

Jenkins, Harold (ed.): *Hamlet* (The Arden Shakespeare), London 1982 (1995).

Jensen, Ole Lisberg: *The Royal Danish Naval Museum. An introduction to the History of the Royal Danish Navy*, Copenhagen 1954.

Klem, Knud: *Helsingør. Vandringer i by og egn*, Copenhagen 1972.

Korse, Poul: *Hollandske spor i nutidens Helsingør*, Elsinore 1994.

Kroman, Erik (ed.):*Danmarks Gamle Købstad-lovgivning*, I–VI, vol. III *Sjælland, Lolland, Falster, Møn, Fyn og Langeland*, Copenhagen 1955.

Kökeritz, Helge: *Shakespeare's Names. A Pronouncing Dictionary*, Yale 1959.

Langberg, Harald: *Kronborg. Vejledning for slottets gæster*, Copenhagen 1979.

– *Dansesalen på Kronborg* (with an appendix in English), Copenhagen 1985.

Lauring, Palle: *A History of the Kingdom of Denmark*, translated by David Hohnen, Copenhagen 1960 (1999).

Leth, André: *Kronborg. Slottet og de kongelige sale*, Copenhagen 1978.

Liisberg, B.: "'Hans Billedgyder' og figurerne paa Kronborgfontainen m.m.", *Kunstmuseets Aarsskrift* 1921–1923, Copenhagen 1924.

Madsen, Lars Bjørn: *Sundtoldstidens Helsingør*, Elsinore 1996.

Mikkelsen, Birger: *Helsingør. Sundtoldstad og borgerby*, Elsinore 1976.

– and Bjørn-Petersen, Elisabeth: *Kronborg*, Elsinore 1977.

Molesworth, Robert: *An Account of Denmark as It was in the Year 1692*, London 1694, (facsimile ed.) Copenhagen 1976.

Olsen, Gunnar (*et al.*): *De danske Stræder og Øresundstolden*, Copenhagen 1958.

Olsen, Olaf (ed.): *Gyldendal og Politikens Danmarkshistorie*, I–XIII, Copenhagen 1988–91.

Olsson, Yngve B.: "In Search of Yorick's Skull: Notes on the Background of *Hamlet*", *Shakespeare Studies* IV, 1968 pp. 183–220.

Pedersen, Kenno: *Det florissante Helsingør*, Elsinore 1991.

– *William Shakespeares Helsingør*, Elsinore 1996.

– *Christian den Fjerdes Helsingør*, Elsinore 1996.

– *Jean Jacob Claessens Helsingør*, Elsinore 1996.

– *Mads Christian Holms Helsingør*, Elsinore 1996.

– *H.C.Andersens Helsingør*, Elsinore 1996.

– and Madsen, Lars Bjørn, in Poul Korse (ed.): *Marienlyst Slot*, Elsinore 1992.

Pedersen, Laurits: *Helsingør*, Copenhagen 1912.

– *Shakespeare og Helsingør*, Copenhagen 1916.

– *Kronborg Have*, Elsinore 1920.

– *Helsingør i Sundtoldstiden 1426–1857*, ed. and author of several chapters, I–II, Copenhagen 1926; also *Tillæg I* (Index) 1931 and *Tillæg II* (Sources) 1992.

Praz, Mario : "Shakespeare's Italy", *Shakespeare Survey 7*, Cambridge 1954.

Saxo Grammaticus: *Danmarks Krønike*, Danish translation by Fr. Winkel Horn, Foreword by Palle Lauring, Copenhagen 1975 (1977).

– *The History of the Danes*, English translation by Peter Fisher, ed. Hilda Ellis Davidsen, I–II, Totowa, N.J. 1980/Cambridge 1979–80.

Schoenbaum, S.: *Shakespeare's Lives*, Oxford & New York 1970.

– *William Shakespeare. A Documentary Life*, Oxford 1975.

Sjögren, Gunnar: *Strövtåg i Shakespeares värld*, Stockholm 1962.

– "The Danish Background in Hamlet", *Shakespeare Studies* IV, 1968 pp. 221–30.

– *Hamlet the Dane*, Lund 1983.

Sløk, Johannes: *Hamlet, prins af Danmark*, Danish translation with notes and a commentary, Copenhagen 1971.

Troels-Lund, Troels: *Dagligt Liv i Norden i det sekstende Aarhundrede*, I–VII, Copenhagen 1879–1901 (1968).

Uhre, Jan: *Øresund og Skibene*, Stenstrup 1997

Wanscher, Vilhelm: *Kronborgs Historie*, Copenhagen 1939.

Wilson, J. Dover: *What Happens in Hamlet*, Cambridge 1935 (1995).

Woldbye, Vibeke and Ole Woldbye: *Kronborg*, Copenhagen 1994.

Zimmerling, Dieter: *Die Hanse. Handelsmacht im Zeichen der Kogge*, Düsseldorf 1976.

Ørnø, Sven: *Good Night, Sweet Prince/Godnat, min prins*, Elsinore 1996.

Østerberg, Valdemar: *Hamlet*, Danish translation with notes and a commentary, Copenhagen 1900–02 (1969).

– "Hamlets Helsingør", *Tilskueren*, XXXVII, 1920, pp. 161–80.

Index